MYRA WALDO'S ROUND·THE·WORLD DIET COOKBOOK

Illustrated by Mike McIver

THE MACMILLAN COMPANY · NEW YORK

COLLIER-MACMILLAN LIMITED · LONDON

Contents

Introduction

Going—and staying—on a diet is a tiresome affair. Anyone
who tells you differently is not being candid or honest.

Most people are completely bored with cottage cheese,
skim milk, lettuce and other diet foods. This book is intended
to make weight reduction, or weight control, a somewhat
pleasanter state of affairs by offering some relief from the
monotony of a diet. And you can experience the vicarious
pleasure of a trip around the world at the same time!

Americans are the most overweight people in the world. This
is largely caused by the fact that we have more food available, at
lower prices, than any other country. In other parts of the world
being overweight is a much less important problem, and
comparatively few people seem to be troubled by excessive
weight. In some measure this is a result of less available food
in relation to income. In addition, however, other countries
tend to cook in a somewhat different fashion from Americans,
and their native dishes are generally less fattening than ours.

In this book you will find the typical dishes of many
countries; all of them are comparatively low in calories.
In losing weight, or in maintaining existing weight, these
foreign recipes will be of considerable assistance. Many of
them are unusual, as well as ideal for weight-reduction diets.

You'll find that dieting is much less difficult if your menus are
interesting. These recipes should help to divert you from the
tiresome, routine foods that all dieters have learned to abhor.
Sheer boredom presents the greatest danger to remaining on a diet.

Be sure to remember to control your portions. The
calorie count set forth at the end of each recipe is based upon
the number of available servings, so please adhere to them.

MYRA WALDO

What You Should Know About Sugar Substitutes

You may use any type of noncaloric sweetener in coffee or tea. However, for cooking, it is advisable to use those made with sodium or calcium cyclamate. For baking, a new type of sugar substitute is now available, and no table of equivalents is required because it can be used, spoon-for-spoon, as a replacement for sugar. This product, under several brand names, is marketed as *low-calorie granulated sugar replacement,* or as *low-calorie table sugar replacement.* It looks exactly like sugar, tastes much like sugar, but has only about three calories a teaspoon rather than the usual eighteen calories found in regular sugar. This substitute is perfect for baking, although it may be used equally well in cooking, using the same amount of sugar substitute as sugar. The most readily available brands are Scoop, Sprinkle Sweet, and Sugar Twin.

A word of caution. For the DESSERT recipes in this book, be absolutely sure the sugar substitute is of the granulated spoon-for-spoon type described above; that is, the label on the container should read "low-calorie granulated sugar replacement," or "low-calorie table sugar replacement." There are other satisfactory noncaloric sweeteners on the market, but they are of a different type, and are usually more concentrated. These are unsatisfactory for baking or making desserts, because they lack the necessary body. With the new spoon-for-spoon sugar replacements, it is now possible to enjoy cakes, cookies, in fact, almost all desserts without a feeling of guilt, even though you're on a diet.

Myra Waldo's
Simple Rules To Diet By

When lunching or dining out in a restaurant, order broiled fish, broiled chicken, small steaks or hamburgers. Remember, however, that a restaurant-sized steak may weigh as much as a pound, and that means fifteen hundred calories, far too many for any diet.

Don't eat between meals, or just before retiring. If you get hungry—and you probably will!—have a cup of coffee or tea, sweetened artificially. If regular coffee is too stimulating at night, have de-caffeinated coffee.

Limit your intake of alcohol. One ounce of most liquors has about one hundred calories, which is quite a good deal. If you have a drink with a mixer, make sure it's one of the noncaloric types. Try, instead of a cocktail or highball before dinner, a glass of dry red or white wine with the meal. Many researchers have found that this actually helps in weight reduction.

Walk around for five minutes, before and after meals. This will help to stimulate your metabolism.

Most important—learn to limit the *amount* you eat. Don't be a member of the Clean Plate Club.

AND, before you eat, stop and think—are you *really* hungry Or is it just part of a pattern of eating at regular times?

No one can diet for you. You have to do it yourself, but the recipes in this book will help make it a nonboring and rewarding experience.

Argentina

Crowned, courted and cooked to perfection, steak reigns king in Argentina. No wonder. The excellence of Argentinian beef elevates that prime cut into a hard-to-resist category. So popular is steak here that until recently restaurants in Buenos Aires often served it with the meal whether ordered or not! Chickens roasted on a spit are another feature. That aforementioned lovely city boasts much good cuisine and sophistication. Dinner starts, more often than not, at 11 P.M. and is long and leisurely. In the interior one often samples the excellent national dish *puchero criollo*, which is a beef (naturally) and vegetable boiled dinner. Particularly unusual is the cold marinated chicken, a piquant dish, slightly Spanish in origin and a specialty of the country.

Marinated Chicken SERVES 6 *250 calories per serving*

4 onions, sliced thin
6 breasts of chicken
2 cloves garlic, minced
2 pimentos, sliced thin
1 stalk celery, chopped
3 tablespoons chopped parsley
⅓ cup tarragon vinegar

¾ cup dry white wine
2 tablespoons olive or vegetable oil
2 teaspoons salt
½ teaspoon pepper
⅛ teaspoon dried ground red peppers
2 bay leaves

Place half the onions in an earthenware or other heatproof casserole (not metal). Arrange the chicken over them and cover with the remaining onions, the garlic, pimentos, celery and parsley.

Combine the vinegar, wine, oil, salt, pepper, red peppers and bay leaves. Add to the casserole. Bring to a boil, cover and cook over medium heat 35 minutes, or until chicken is tender.

Chill for 24 hours and serve cold.

Australia

The country-continent Australia's kitchen-cauldron is a melting pot of English and European influences. English is still the strongest influence but as more Europeans enter the country, culinary customs and habits are changing. Three hearty meals (and lots to drink) are on the daily food agenda. Energy is needed to keep the hard-working Australians on the go. Meats—lamb and beef in particular—are favorite main dishes, for unlike their English forefathers, the Australians have an abundance of both. Seafood, particularly in the big coastal cities, is excellent. Desserts tend to be simple English derivatives—favorites like crumpets, scones and biscuits are served at teatime.

Marinated Beef

2 teaspoons salt
¾ teaspoon pepper
1 teaspoon paprika
2 cloves garlic, minced
3 pounds sirloin of beef
½ cup dry red wine
¼ cup wine vinegar

3 onions, chopped
3 tomatoes, peeled and
chopped
2 green peppers, chopped
1 bay leaf
¼ pound mushrooms,
sliced

Combine the salt, pepper, paprika and garlic; rub into the meat thoroughly. Mix the wine and vinegar together and pour over the meat in a bowl. Marinate in the refrigerator overnight, basting and turning the meat a few times.

Remove the meat from the refrigerator 3 hours before it is to be roasted. Drain the meat, reserving the marinade. Place the meat on a rack in a shallow roasting pan.

Roast in a 475° oven 20 minutes; pour off the fat. Reduce the heat to 350° and add the onions, tomatoes, green peppers, bay leaf, mushrooms and reserved marinade. Roast an additional 35 minutes for rare, 40 for medium and 50 for well done.

Discard the bay leaf, skim off the fat and force the gravy and vegetables through a sieve, or puree in a blender.

† Serve 2 slices, ¼ inch thick and 2 tablespoons gravy per portion.

Austria

Why is teatime always coffee time in Vienna? Easy. Into strong coffee goes *Schlagobers*—mounds of rich, puffy whipped cream—and you just can't do that with tea. Also on the menu is a marvelous assortment of flaky pastries, tortes and cakes. Teatime is not diet time in Austria! The history of empire is incorporated into its cuisine—cheese dishes from Switzerland, pastas from Italy, paprikas and stuffed cabbage rolls from Hungary. Austrians love boiled beef, and many restaurants make a charming lunchtime specialty of it. This is served with an assortment of relishes, and soon everything is gorgeously *gemütlich* (warm and happy), as are most meals in Austria.

Stuffed Cabbage Rolls   SERVES 6   *280 calories per serving*

1 large head cabbage
3 onions
Veal knuckles or bones
1 29-ounce can
   tomatoes
1 pound ground lean beef
3 teaspoons salt
1/4 teaspoon black pepper

1/2 cup rice, half-cooked
   and drained
1 egg, beaten
2 tablespoons cold water
4 tablespoons lemon juice
1 tablespoon brown sugar
2 tablespoons low calorie
   granulated sugar
   replacement*

Cover the whole cabbage with water; bring to a boil and cook 10 minutes. Drain. Carefully separate 12 leaves.

Slice 2 onions and combine in a large heavy saucepan with the bones and tomatoes. Cook over medium heat while preparing the cabbage rolls.

Grate the remaining onion and combine with the beef, 1 1/2 teaspoons salt, the pepper, rice, egg and water. Mix well. Place a heaping tablespoon of the mixture on each leaf. Turn two opposite sides in and carefully roll up the cabbage. They should stay rolled up, but if not, fasten with toothpicks or tie with thread.

Arrange rolls in the tomato mixture (if there is any meat mixture left, form into balls and add). Add the remaining salt. Cover and cook over low heat 1 hour. Stir in the lemon juice, brown sugar and sugar replacement. Cook uncovered 30 minutes. Taste for seasoning; it should be both sweet and sour. Skim the fat.

* See page 5.

Belgium

A small country, Belgium neighbors France, and it might seem that its cuisine would be lost to the wonders of the formidable French. On the contrary. Belgium has developed its own fine table, influenced in some part by its neighbors, but nevertheless distinctly national. Soups are in high esteem, and *waterzoie* is a stew-soup (so thick it's hard to tell which) made with either chicken or fish, but low in calories. A delectable main course incorporating beer (the national drink) is *carbonnade à la Flamande*—small slices of beef in a hearty, rich beer sauce. The famous endive, a prize salad ingredient, is exported throughout the world, as are the big and beautiful Belgian black grapes. Cheeses are popular for dessert and if the sweet tooth demands, delicious tarts and pastries are usually at hand. But we'll just have fruit.

Beef-Beer Casserole   SERVES 6   *375 calories per serving*

1 tablespoon butter or margarine	2 teaspoons vinegar
4 onions, sliced	1½ teaspoons salt
2 pounds beef (chuck, top or bottom round) cut in 12 pieces	½ teaspoon pepper
	½ teaspoon low calorie granulated sugar replacement*
2 teaspoons flour	2 bay leaves
1 cup beer	½ teaspoon thyme
	3 tablespoons chopped parsley

Melt the butter in a heavy saucepan or casserole; sauté the onions 10 minutes, stirring frequently. Remove the onions. Brown the beef on all sides; sprinkle with the flour, stirring until well blended. Return the onions to the pan and add the beer, vinegar, salt, pepper, sugar replacement, bay leaves, thyme and parsley. Cover and cook over low heat 2 hours. Stir occasionally and add a little water if necessary. Skim the fat and serve.

* See page 5.

Waterzoie SERVES 6
(Belgian Chicken in White Wine)

2 2-pound broilers	2 teaspoons salt
Veal bones, chicken feet	½ teaspoon pepper
7 cups water	1 lemon, peeled and sliced
2 stalks celery	thin
1 celery root, peeled and	1 cup dry white wine
sliced	1 tablespoon butter
4 sprigs parsley	½ cup dry bread crumbs

Have the broilers left whole. Ask the butcher for a veal knuckle, some additional veal bones, and chicken feet for the stock.

Combine the livers, gizzards and hearts of the broilers, the bones, water, celery, celery root, parsley, salt, pepper and lemon in a saucepan. Bring to a boil and skim the top. Cover and cook over medium heat for 2 hours. Strain the stock and skim off the fat.

In a casserole, place the broilers, stock, wine and butter. Cover and cook over low heat 45 minutes, or until the broilers are tender. Remove the chicken and cut into individual servings. Stir the bread crumbs into the soup. Serve the chicken and soup together in deep plates or bowls.

Brazil

The first food Brazil brings to mind is unquestionably coffee. Truly the national drink, strong and sweet, it is sipped from morning to night in tiny cups. What does one eat in the land of coffee? Brazil offers an interesting cuisine with definite Portuguese influences. *Feijoada,* a bean dish containing meat, rice, and spices, is probably the most popular national recipe, and has many variations. Shrimps are excellent, and two of the most famous ways of preparation are barbecued and sizzling on a spit, or baked into little pies called *empadinhas de camarão.* For breakfast Brazilians have coffee, of course, and little else. A large lunch is followed by a late dinner. In between, it's coffee—a wonderful way to keep hunger pangs away. Desserts use the local fruits, and the following soufflé is an elegant example.

Orange Soufflé   SERVES 4   *100 calories per serving*

4 ladyfingers
4 eggs, separated
¼ teaspoon salt

⅔ cup low calorie granulated
sugar replacement*
2 teaspoons orange extract

Preheat the oven to 350°.

Separate the ladyfingers, and arrange half of the pieces on the bottom of a lightly oiled 1-quart soufflé dish.

Beat the egg yolks in a bowl; add the salt, sugar replacement and orange extract. Beat until thickened and light in color. Beat the egg whites until stiff but not dry; carefully fold them into the yolk mixture. Pour half the mixture into the soufflé dish. Arrange the remaining ladyfingers over it, and pour the remaining soufflé mixture over the second layer of ladyfingers. Place the soufflé dish in a shallow pan of hot water and bake in a preheated 350° oven for 35 minutes, or until the soufflé is puffed and set. Serve immediately.

* See page 5.

Brazilian Fish Casserole SERVES 6 *275 calories per serving*

2 soles, filleted
2 teaspoons salt
½ teaspoon freshly ground
    black pepper
1 teaspoon ground
    coriander
2 cups tomatoes,
    peeled and chopped

½ cup sliced green onions
1 bay leaf, finely crumbled
¼ cup parsley
3 cups water
    Dash cayenne pepper
1½ pounds uncooked shrimp,
    shelled and deveined

Cut the fish into slices about ¾-inch thick, reserving the head of the fish. Rub the slices with a mixture of the salt, pepper, and coriander; place in a glass or pottery bowl and add the tomatoes, green onions, bay leaf, and parsley. Cover and let stand in the refrigerator 2 hours.

Combine the fish head and water in a casserole; bring to a boil and cook over medium heat 30 minutes. Discard the head and add the fish mixture. Bring to a boil, cover, and cook over low heat 35 minutes. Add the cayenne pepper and shrimp; cook 10 minutes longer. Taste for seasoning.

Canada

Like the United States, Canada stretches from Atlantic to Pacific; unlike the United States, where so many mixtures of nationalities have dominated the cuisine, only two major influences are felt here: English and French. Fish in Canada, caught from either coast, is excellent. Gaspé salmon from the east and Coho from the west are extraordinary, as are the shrimp, lobster and crabs. Canadian bacon is unequaled and is exported throughout the world. This is also true for their delicious Cheddar cheese. The French influence is strong in Quebec, where local specialties include *soupe aux pois Canadienne,* a filling, hearty pea soup, locally grown cabbage used as a vegetable and in soup, and *ragoût de boulettes,* stew with ground pork balls. In Ontario and Alberta, on the other hand, roast beef and Yorkshire pudding rate high. Canadian apples, like most of their fruits and vegetables, are of top quality and served frequently with meals and as dessert.

Baked Apple   SERVES 6   *125 calories per serving*

6 baking apples
½ cup low calorie granulated
  sugar replacement*
1 tablespoon butter or margarine

1 teaspoon cinnamon
6 drops red food coloring
¼ cup dry white wine
¼ cup water

Wash, dry and core the apples. Pare off a little of the skin from the top of each apple. Put the sugar replacement in the cored apples, and arrange them in a baking pan.

Combine the butter, cinnamon, red food coloring, wine and water in a saucepan. Bring to a boil, and pour over the apples. Bake in a 375° oven 45 minutes, or until apples are tender, basting frequently. Cool.

* See page 5.

Cream of Cabbage Soup   SERVES 8   *8o calories per serving*

1 tablespoon butter
1 cup sliced onions
1½ cups peeled sliced potatoes
1½ pounds cabbage, shredded
6 cups chicken broth
    (skimmed of fat)

1 teaspoon salt
½ teaspoon white pepper
½ cup milk
    paprika

Melt the butter in a saucepan. Add the onions, potatoes and cabbage. Cover and cook over low heat 10 minutes, shaking the pan frequently. Add the broth, salt and pepper; cover again and cook 30 minutes longer. Puree the mixture in an electric blender or force through a sieve. Return to the saucepan; mix in the milk. Heat and taste for seasoning. Serve sprinkled with paprika.

Ceylon

Ceylon's cuisine resembles that of India, but with certain important agricultural and seasoning differences. A combination of powdered Maldive fish, red chili peppers, ginger, onions, and garlic (a very spicy conglomerate) provides the prime seasoning source. Most meats, vegetables, fish and poultry dishes are prepared with curry as a seasoning, as well as a host of rare fruits, leaves and flowers. Sweetmeats are popular, but for dessert the selection of exotic fruits is fresh and unusual. As one expects, tea is the favored drink, and the quality of that beverage is excellent.

Spiced Chicken   SERVES 6   *200 calories per serving*

1 cup buttermilk or yogurt
1 clove garlic, minced
2 2½-pound fryers, disjointed
2 tablespoons butter or
    margarine

2 onions, chopped fine
1½ teaspoons salt
½ teaspoon powdered ginger
1 tablespoon curry powder
1 teaspoon cornstarch

Mix the buttermilk and garlic in a bowl. Add the chickens and let marinate 2 hours. Baste and turn frequently.

Melt the butter in a deep skillet or casserole; sauté the onions 10 minutes, stirring frequently. Sprinkle with the salt, ginger, curry powder and cornstarch, stirring until well blended. Drain the chicken (reserve the buttermilk) and cook in skillet until chicken is lightly browned. Stir in the buttermilk. Cover and cook over moderate heat just to the boiling point. Transfer to 350° oven for ½ hour, or until chicken is tender.

Chile

Its water and mountain forests give Chile foodstuffs that have enabled its people to develop one of the most highly sophisticated and delectable cuisines in South America. With the Pacific, and a cold-water current running alongside its 2,600 mile coastal shoreline, Chile boasts exquisite fish and seafood, some species exclusively its own. Its national dish, *chupe,* is a seafood chowder prepared either mild or spicy depending on the individual cook's taste and treasured family recipe. From the interior, game birds are abundant and these are delicately prepared, often in wine—another product of which Chile can boast. Dinner is eaten quite late, and to stave off hunger pangs a 5:30 tea (really a light meal) and a 6:30 vermouth hour are the relaxing custom.

Chilean Fish Stew SERVES 6 *220 calories per serving*

3 tomatoes, chopped, or
   1 cup canned, drained
2 cloves garlic, minced
3 onions, sliced
2 green peppers, cut
   julienne fashion
2 teaspoons paprika
$\frac{1}{4}$ teaspoon saffron
2 tablespoons olive oil

6 slices (2 pounds) fish
   (sea bass, snapper, pike)
$2\frac{1}{2}$ teaspoons salt
2 bay leaves
$\frac{1}{4}$ teaspoon dried ground red
   pepper
$1\frac{1}{2}$ cups dry white wine
$1\frac{1}{2}$ cups water
$\frac{1}{2}$ cup uncooked rice

In a saucepan, cook the tomatoes and garlic for 10 minutes over low heat. Mash until smooth, then add the onions, green peppers, paprika and saffron. Cook over low heat 15 minutes, stirring frequently.

Heat the oil in a casserole or Dutch oven; brown the fish in it on both sides. Add the salt, bay leaves, red peppers, wine, water and tomato mixture. Bring to a boil and add the rice. Cover and cook over low heat 25 minutes. Taste for seasoning and serve hot.

China

A country that throughout its history had scarcely enough food to feed its people developed one of the world's finest cuisines. They did it with economy, flair and a highly individual way of preparation and serving. Four provinces in the vast expanse of China have most influenced its cookery: Canton (most popular here, emphasizing dishes fried quickly in a wok); Honan, specializing in sweet-and-sour sauces; Szechuan, with hot and spicy dishes; and Fukien, where soups and stewlike dishes are distinctive. Tea is served almost exclusively as the beverage, and, of course, rice is the mainstay of the diet.

Lo Mein   SERVES 6   *220 calories per serving*

2 tablespoons peanut oil
2 onions, sliced
¾ pound mushrooms, sliced
2 cups sliced celery
1½ cups chicken broth
1 cup bean sprouts
1 cup water chestnuts, sliced

½ cup bamboo shoots, sliced
3 tablespoons soy sauce
1 tablespoon cornstarch
3 cups sliced cooked chicken (or turkey)
3 cups cooked fine egg noodles

Heat the oil in a skillet. Add the onions and sauté 10 minutes, stirring frequently. Add the mushrooms, celery and broth, cook over low heat 5 minutes. Add the bean sprouts, water chestnuts and bamboo shoots and cook 3 minutes more. Mix the soy sauce and cornstarch. When smooth, add to the skillet and cook, stirring constantly, until thickened. Mix in the chicken and heat through. Correct seasoning. Serve on the noodles.

Shrimp and Green Peas   SERVES 6   *165 calories per serving*

2 tablespoons vegetable oil
1½ pounds raw shrimp, shelled and cleaned
3 green onions, sliced thin
1-inch piece fresh ginger or 1½ teaspoons powdered ginger
2 cloves garlic, minced
1 cup canned tiny green peas, drained
2 teaspoons cornstarch
1 teaspoon salt
1 teaspoon low calorie granulated sugar replacement*
2 teaspoons soy sauce
½ cup cold water

Heat the oil in a skillet; lightly brown the shrimp on both sides. Add the onions, ginger, garlic and peas. Cook over low heat 2 minutes.

Mix the cornstarch, salt, sugar replacement, soy sauce and water until smooth; pour over the shrimp mixture. Stir constantly to the boiling point; cook 2 minutes. Taste for seasoning and serve immediately.

* See page 5.

Colombia

Orchids, emeralds, exotic fruit, a Caribbean coastline, another on the Pacific, and a beautiful capital high in the mountains can give one an idea of the flavor to be found in Colombia. And cooking flavor? That's spicy. Staple food? That's corn. In between is a whole range of distinctive dishes. Among these are *sopa de maíz* (corn soup), *cocido Bogotana* (beef stew with vegetables and small pieces of corn on the cob), *pastel de maíz* (delicious corn pie). A lovely custom here is a festive Sunday breakfast. *Tamal* (a cornmeal mixture, wrapped and steamed) is the great specialty and is eaten with hot chocolate, bread and cheese. The local fruit is excellent, unusual and sometimes made into delicious ice cream. Of course, coffee is served everywhere, and also used as a flavoring in desserts.

Mocha Cream   SERVES 6   *100 calories per serving*

1 teaspoon gelatin
1 tablespoon cold water
1½ squares unsweetened
   chocolate
⅓ cup hot water
2 eggs, separated
2 teaspoons instant coffee

¾ cup low calorie granu-
   lated sugar replacement*
½ teaspoon salt
½ teaspoon cinnamon
¼ cup sifted flour
2⅔ cups skim milk
¼ teaspon cream of tartar

Sprinkle the gelatin into the cold water and set aside. Melt the chocolate in a small pan, placed in a larger pan of boiling water. Add hot water to chocolate and stir until smooth.

Lightly beat the egg yolks in the top of a double boiler, then stir in the instant coffee, ⅔ cup sugar replacement, the salt, cinnamon and flour. Beat in the milk until smooth, then add the chocolate. Place over hot water and cook, stirring constantly, for 10 minutes, or until thickened. Stir in the gelatin until dissolved. Place the pan in ice water until cold, then turn into a 1-quart baking dish.

While the chocolate mixture is cooking, beat together the egg whites, cream of tartar and remaining sugar replacement until mixture is stiff but not dry. Heap on top of the chocolate mixture. Place on the upper level of a preheated 375° oven for 10 minutes, or until the top is delicately browned. Cool, and serve at room temperature.

* See page 5.

Czechoslovakia

An old-time meal in Czechoslovakia rarely begins with an appetizer—soup is the start, thick and rich. Then, possibly, *ryba na černo,* a freshwater fish dish covered with a delicious black sauce—many ingredients but worth the effort. Ham, sausages, roast pork and dumplings *(knedlíky)* of all sizes and shapes provide the backbone of main-course cookery. Another dish, *vařené hovězí maso* (boiled beef), is served amid a variety of delicious sauces. Sauerkraut, unquestionably the national vegetable, appears at the table prepared with many seasonings, and added ingredients for extra flavor. Goose, available from the forests of Bohemia, is another specialty, and all this is accompanied by beer, the national drink, which reaches great excellence in the country's Pilsener product—light, delicate and crystal clear. Desserts feature poppy seeds, fruits and nuts.

Paprika Soup   SERVES 6   *85 calories per serving*

½ pound chuck beef
1½ teaspoons low calorie granu-
    lated sugar replacement*
1 teaspoon flour
1 green pepper, sliced
2 tomatoes, peeled and chopped

1½ teaspoons salt
½ teaspoon freshly ground
    black pepper
2 teaspoons paprika
1 teaspoon caraway seeds
6 cups beef broth

Trim all the fat off the meat and cut the beef into ½-inch cubes. Heat a Dutch oven or heavy saucepan and rub it with a piece of fat speared on a fork. Put the beef cubes in the pan, cover and brown on all sides over medium heat, watching carefully to prevent them from sticking and burning. Sprinkle the meat with the sugar replacement and flour and brown well. Add the green pepper, tomatoes, salt, black pepper, paprika, seeds and broth. Cover and cook over low heat 1½ hours or until very tender. Correct seasoning, and skim off any fat.

* See page 5.

Nut Torte   SERVES 12   *with cream, 160 calories per serving*
without cream, 120 calories per serving

4 eggs, separated
¾ cup low calorie granu-
    lated sugar replacement*

1 teaspoon baking powder
¾ cup ground walnuts
1 cup dried fine bread crumbs

Grease and lightly dust with flour an 8-inch spring-form cake pan or two 8-inch layer-cake pans. Preheat oven to 375°.

Beat the egg yolks and gradually add half the sugar replacement, beating until light and thick. Lightly beat in the baking powder, walnuts and crumbs.

Beat the egg whites until they form peaks, then slowly add the remaining sugar replacement and continue beating until stiff. Fold into the nut mixture. Turn into the pan or pans.

Bake, allowing 30 minutes for the spring-form, or 20 minutes for the layer-cake pans, or until a cake tester comes out clean when inserted in the center. Cool 10 minutes on a cake rack. Spread layers with fluffy whipped cream (see recipe below), or dust with confectioners' sugar.

Fluffy Whipped Cream   MAKES ABOUT 3 CUPS
490 calories in all

3 egg whites
1 tablespoon low calorie granu-
    lated sugar replacement*

½ cup heavy cream,
    whipped
½ teaspoon vanilla extract

Beat the egg whites until stiff, then beat in the sugar replacement. Fold the heavy cream and vanilla into the egg whites.

* See page 5.

Denmark

There is nothing harder to resist than the sight of a *smørrebød* display in Copenhagen. The Danes have perfected the art of making the open sandwich—the *smørrebød* sandwich. Open sandwiches save a slice of bread—a good idea, when watching calories. Food quality is of the highest here, and into their *smørrebød* goes thin slices of the freshest varieties of bread, sweet butter, tiny "just-caught" shrimps, slices of hard-cooked eggs, herrings, meat slices, and garnishes that look as if they came from an artist's palette rather than the marketplace. Add to this their original world-famous pastry, a gift for adapting "continental" cuisine, and it's easy to see why Denmark is a food perfectionist's haven.

Sweet and Sour Red Cabbage   SERVES 6   *65 calories per serving*

3 pounds red cabbage, shredded
2 tablespoons butter or margarine
4 tablespoons vinegar
½ cup water
2 tablespoons currant jelly
1½ teaspoons salt
3 tablespoons low calorie granulated sugar replacement*

Drain the cabbage. Melt the margarine in a heavy saucepan. Add the cabbage and toss to coat with the margarine. Add the vinegar and water. Cover and cook over low heat 1 hour. Add the jelly, salt and sugar replacement; cook 30 minutes longer. Taste for seasoning. Serve with main courses.

* See page 5.

Baked Lettuce SERVES 6   *55 calories per serving*

2 heads lettuce
1 tablespoon cornstarch
¼ cup milk
1 cup canned chicken broth
1 teaspoon salt

1 tablespoon butter or
    margarine
2 tablespoons coarsely
    chopped nuts
2 tablespoons dry bread crumbs

Wash the lettuce and remove any bruised leaves. Pour boiling water over it, let soak 1 minute, then drain. Cook in water to cover 5 minutes; drain very well. Cut each head in 3. Place in a casserole.

Mix the cornstarch and milk until smooth in a saucepan. Stir in the broth, salt and butter. Cook over low heat, stirring constantly until the boiling point. Pour over the lettuce and sprinkle with the bread crumbs and nuts.

Bake in 425° oven 15 minutes or until browned.

Bacon-and-Egg Pancake SERVES 6   *105 calories per serving*

6 slices bacon
4 eggs
1 tablespoon flour
½ teaspoon salt

1 cup skim milk
2 tablespoons
    minched chives or
    green onions

Cut the bacon in half, crosswise. Using a 12-inch skillet, fry the bacon until browned, but not crisp. Drain on paper towels.

Pour off all but 1 tablespoon of the fat. Beat together the eggs, flour, salt and milk. Reheat the skillet, and pour in the egg mixture. Bake in a preheated 325° oven 12 minutes. Arrange the bacon on top, and bake 3 minutes longer, or until the mixture is set. Don't overcook. Sprinkle with the chives or green onions, and serve, cut into wedges. This dish is excellent for luncheon, or as a supper dish.

Ecuador

On the equator but blessed with mountains, Ecuador has two starkly different climates—and cooks accordingly. In the steamy lowlands, light food and cool drinks are a necessity. In the mountains, where a perpetually springlike atmosphere prevails, a more elaborate cuisine has developed. Fruits are exquisite here, and much is done with them. Desserts usually are a type of rice or fruit pudding, or fresh fruit. The *naranjilla,* a type of orange with a bright green interior makes a delicious juice, but also ends up as ice cream that is an unparalleled treat. Soups are rated high and *locro* and *ajiaco* are two vegetable varieties made with potatoes and corn. *Ajís,* spicy dishes, are the most popular main courses and are most often prepared with chicken and shrimp as the major ingredients.

Chicken, Hunter's Style   SERVES 6   *150 calories per serving*

3 tablespoons flour	1 onion, chopped
1½ teaspoons salt	2 cups canned tomatoes
½ teaspoon pepper	1 green pepper, coarsely
1 4-pound roasting chicken,	chopped
disjointed	¼ teaspoon dried oregano
1 tablespoon olive oil	¼ cup dry white wine

Mix the flour, salt and pepper together; lightly roll the chicken in the mixture. Heat the oil in a deep skillet; sauté the onion and chicken until well browned. Add the tomatoes, green pepper, oregano and wine. Cover and cook over low heat 50 minutes, or until the chicken is tender. Skim the fat, then taste for seasoning.

Meringue Rice Pudding   SERVES 6   *155 calories per serving*

½ cup rice
2 cups water
¾ teaspoon salt
3 eggs, separated
½ cup low calorie granu-
    lated sugar replacement*

½ teaspoon vanilla
    extract
3 cups skim milk,
    scalded
¼ teaspoon almond
    extract

Wash the rice well and combine in a suacepan with the water and salt. Bring to a boil and cook over low heat 25 minutes. Drain. Preheat oven to 325°.

Beat together the egg yolks, ⅓ cup sugar replacement and vanilla in a saucepan. Gradually add the scalded milk, beating steadily. Cook over low heat, stirring constantly, until the mixture coats the spoon. Add the rice; mix well and turn into a 2-quart baking dish.

Beat the egg whites until stiff but not dry. Beat in the remaining sugar replacement and almond extract. Pile on the rice mixture. Bake 15 minutes. Serve hot or cold.

VARIATION: Use 2 cups double-strength coffee and 1 cup scalded skim milk in place of the 3 cups skim milk. Serves 6 with 135 calories per serving.

* See page 5.

Finland

Finland's cold winter climate keeps visitors from learning about these warm, solid people. Go in summer—weather's glorious; lakes, forests and unspoiled scenery abound. Because of Finland's considerable coast areas, fish is the staple of its cookery. Herring here is akin to flour in other countries—bought in barrels and eaten many times a day prepared in a variety of ways. Like their Scandinavian neighbors, the Finns are partial to *smörgåsbord*, here called *voileipäpöytä*—hard to pronounce but don't let that stop you. The ingredients are fresh and delicious. Mushrooms are a favorite vegetable, and they are prepared in many ways. During the long winter, meat stews are favorites. In the summer all kinds of berries are abundant and delicious; these are served fresh as dessert, or made into fine preserves and stored for winter.

Pickled Herring *60 calories per serving*

6 salt herring fillets
3 onions, sliced
½ cup water
1½ cups white
    vinegar

¼ cup low calorie granu-
    lated sugar replacement*
2 tablespoons pickling spice
2 bay leaves
dill sprigs or dill weed

Wash the herring, and place in a bowl with cold water to cover. Let soak 24 hours, changing the water frequently. Drain well and cut each fillet into 2-inch pieces, crosswise. Put the herring into a glass jar or bowl and cover with the onions.

In a saucepan, combine the water, vinegar, sugar replacement, pickling spice and bay leaves. Bring to a boil, and stir until sugar replacement is dissolved. Pour over the herring. Add a few fresh dill sprigs or a little dill weed. Cover tightly and refrigerate for 48 hours before serving.

* See page 5.

Stuffed Mushrooms MAKES 18 *10 calories in each*

18 mushrooms
1 teaspoon salt
⅛ teaspoon pepper
½ teaspoon paprika

2 tablespoons grated onion
2 tablespoons grated
    cheese
1 teaspoon oil

Buy medium-sized mushrooms. Wash and dry them; remove the stems and chop these fine. Combine with the salt, pepper, paprika, onion and cheese. Mix well and stuff the mushroom caps.

Oil a baking pan and arrange the mushrooms on it. Bake in a 375° oven 10 minutes. Spear with cocktail picks and serve hot.

France

The food history of exquisite cuisine in all the Western world is inexorably tied to the great culinary history of France. From France come the superb sauces, great chefs, vintage wines, fabulous cheeses, mouth-watering desserts, and beautiful brandies. To be necessarily (if unfortunately) brief, there are basically two types of French cooking, *bourgeoise* (middle class) and *haute cuisine,* the latter the traditional style of the great chefs. Both are delicious—*haute cuisine* usually quite elaborate, *bourgeoise* less so but with favorites sometimes quite time-consuming to prepare. Paris is the center of *haute cuisine,* but great restaurants can be found in every province. To hear a Frenchman argue with another about which region or province rates as culinary best in France gives one an understanding of why dining here is pedestal-placed, and nothing short of the excellence demanded by its gourmets—numbering practically the entire population!

Chicken Marengo SERVES 6 *180 calories per serving*

3 tablespoons flour
2 teaspoons salt
½ teaspoon pepper
2 2-pound chickens,
    disjointed
1 tablespoon olive oil
1 tablespoon cognac
2 cloves garlic, minced
1 stalk celery

2 sprigs parsley
1 bay leaf
½ teaspoon dried thyme
2 tomatoes, peeled and diced
1 cup dry white wine
½ pound mushrooms,
    cut in quarters
2 tablespoons chopped
    parsley

Mix the flour, salt and pepper together; lightly roll the chicken in the mixture.

Heat the olive oil in a skillet; brown the chicken in it. Transfer to a casserole; heat the cognac, pour it over the chicken and set it aflame. When the flames die, add the garlic, celery, parsley, bay leaf, thyme, tomatoes and wine. Cover and cook over low heat 30 minutes. Add the mushrooms and cook 15 minutes longer or until the chicken is tender. Taste for seasoning; remove the celery, parsley and bay leaf. Sprinkle with the parsley and serve directly from the casserole.

Scallop Ramekins SERVES 6   *140 calories per serving*

1 pound scallops
1 cup dry white wine
¼ teaspoon thyme
1 stalk celery
2 sprigs parsley
1 bay leaf
1 teaspoon salt
½ pound mushrooms,
    chopped
1 onion, chopped

1 tablespoon chopped
    parsley
1 tablespoon butter
2 tablespoons water
1 teaspoon lemon juice
½ teaspoon pepper
1 tablespoon flour
1 egg yolk
3 tablespoons milk
paprika

Wash and drain the scallops; combine the wine, thyme, celery, parsley and bay leaf in a saucepan. Bring to a boil and add the scallops and salt. Cook over low heat 5 minutes. Strain the stock and cut the scallops in small pieces. Reserve the stock.

Combine the mushrooms, onion, parsley, butter, water, lemon juice and pepper in a saucepan; cover and cook over low heat 10 minutes. Stir in the flour, and gradually add the reserved stock. Cook 2 minutes, stirring constantly.

Beat the egg yolk and milk in a bowl; gradually add the mushroom mixture, stirring constantly to prevent curdling. Add the scallops and taste for seasoning.

Pile into 6 individual ramekins or shells. Sprinkle with the paprika. Place under a hot broiler until delicately browned. Serve immediately.

Germany

The strapping good health of a smiling, rosy-cheeked *Bürgermeister* symbolizes the good robust food of Germany. Hard workers, Germans have little time for dainty delicacies; more to their taste are the substantially flavored, plate-filling dishes like sauerbraten, sausages and sauerkraut. Breakfast (*Frühstück*), the only exception, is typically continental After that, and all through the day, fulfilling dishes of beef, pork, potatoes and dumplings constitute the backbone of this hearty cuisine—but sauerbraten prepared in the following way lets you enjoy it with no worry about calories.

Sauerbraten   SERVES 8

2 cups white vinegar	2 carrots, sliced
2 teaspoons salt	4 pounds beef
10 peppercorns	(chuck, brisket,
3 cloves	top round)
2 bay leaves	¾ cup boiling water
2 onions, chopped	½ cup yogurt

Bring to a boil the vinegar, salt, peppercorns, cloves, bay leaves, onions and carrots.

Place the meat in an earthenware or glass (non-metal) bowl and pour the marinade over it. Cover the bowl and refrigerate for 3 days, turning the meat frequently. Drain the meat, reserving the marinade.

Brown the meat over low heat in a heavy saucepan or Dutch oven. Add the marinade and water. Cover and cook over low heat 3 hours, or until meat is tender. Skim off the fat. Stir in the yogurt.

† Serve 2 slices, ¼ inch thick, to a portion; 300 calories in each serving. Leftovers are delicious reheated.

Greece

Historically great are Greece's architectural landmarks —historically simple is its cuisine. Basically an agricultural country and not prone to extensive, lavish cooking, it has, nonetheless, some good, well-seasoned dishes under the classic profile. Probably the most popular is *moussaka* (eggplant stuffed with ground lamb), and *entrather* (lamb with artichokes). Beautiful, big lemons are grown in Greece and used as a garnish or ingredient in practically everything. *Soupa avgolemono,* a chicken soup with lemon flavoring, is quite exceptional, filling but low in calories.

Greek Meat Casserole   SERVES 6   *290 calories per serving*

1½ tablespoons olive or salad oil

1½ pounds lean beef, cut in ½-inch cubes

1 eggplant, peeled and sliced thin

2 onions, sliced thin

4 tomatoes, cubed

2 green peppers, diced

2 teaspoons salt

¾ teaspoon pepper

½ teaspoon oregano

Heat 1 tablespoon oil in a skillet; brown the beef in it over high heat.

Grease a casserole with the remaining oil. Arrange successive layers of the eggplant, beef, onions, tomatoes and green peppers, seasoning each layer with a mixture of the salt, pepper and oregano. Cover the casserole.

Bake in a 350° oven 1 hour. Remove the cover and bake 15 minutes longer.

Greek Lamb Mélange SERVES 6 *345 calories per serving*

1½ pounds boneless lamb
1 clove garlic, minced
1 cup diced onions
2 carrots, sliced
2 green peppers, diced
1 cup canned tomato
   sauce
1½ teaspoons salt

½ teaspoon freshly ground
   black pepper
2 teaspoons paprika
2 potatoes, peeled and cubed
½ pound green beans,
   cut in thirds
½ pound green squash,
   peeled and thinly sliced

Trim all the fat from the lamb and cut the meat into 1-inch cubes.

Rub a heated Dutch oven or heavy saucepan with a small piece of the fat. Add the lamb and brown all over. Add the garlic and onions and continue browning, watching carefully to prevent sticking and burning. Add the carrots, green peppers and tomato sauce. Season with the salt, pepper and paprika. Cover and cook over low heat 1 hour. Add the potatoes, beans and squash and cook 30 minutes more, adding a little water if necessary. Taste for seasoning.

Greek Lemon Soup SERVES 8 *90 calories per serving*

¼ cup rice
6 cups chicken broth

2 egg yolks
2 tablespoons lemon juice

Wash the rice in warm water and let soak 15 minutes. Drain. Bring the broth to a boil; add the rice and cook over low heat 15 minutes. Beat the egg yolks and lemon juice in a bowl. Gradually add about 1 cup of the hot broth, stirring constantly to prevent curdling. Return mixture to balance of broth, stirring constantly; taste for seasoning, heat, but do not allow to boil. Serve with a slice of lemon in each plate.

Hungary

Can one stay hungry in Hungary? (Pardon the pun.) Not long. The food's much too appetizing, and the atmosphere is permeated with the love-of-life philosophy of the people. The present form of government has slowed things down a bit, but the Hungarian people are irrepressibly gay, with a love of good food and happy music (particularly of the gypsy variety). Not all cooking here is goulash (proper terminology *gulyás*), but there is a national spice, and that's paprika—sweet or hot variety. Paprika can be found almost everywhere you would expect to find it—in chicken, meats, and cucumbers. But it is found where you wouldn't expect it, too—in bacon and cheeses! Dumplings and noodles are beautifully prepared, as are the sweets and desserts—an array of strudels, tortes and nut cakes.

Mushrooms In Sour Cream   SERVES 6   *45 calories per serving*

1 tablespoon butter or margarine	1 teaspoon salt
1 onion, chopped	¼ teaspoon pepper
1 pound mushrooms, sliced	1 teaspoon paprika
	2 tablespoons sour cream

Melt the butter in a skillet; sauté the onion 5 minutes, stirring frequently. Add the mushrooms and sauté 5 minutes. Season with salt, pepper and paprika; stir in the sour cream. Heat, but do not let boil.

Fish Paprikash   SERVES 6   *165 calories per serving*

1 tablespoon butter or
    margarine
4 onions, chopped
2 teaspoons paprika
6 (2 pounds) slices fish (sea
    bass, lake trout, whitefish)

2 teaspoons salt
½ teaspoon freshly ground
    black pepper
1 cup water
½ cup yogurt or
    buttermilk

Melt the butter in a deep skillet; sauté the onions for 10 minutes, stirring frequently. Blend in the paprika. Arrange the fish over the onions; season with the salt and pepper. Add the water and bring to a boil. Cover and cook over low heat 45 minutes. Taste for seasoning.

Carefully remove the fish to a serving dish. Stir the yogurt into the sauce; heat but do not boil. Pour over the fish and serve.

India

Exotic, mysterious India. Still so. Food—not quite the spicy generalities that one may think. As the picture emerges (with the country's economic difficulties taken into consideration) it becomes clear why vegetables and rice have reached such importance. These are prepared in a myriad of ways, but principally as curries. Curries are made by simply adding a mixture of ground spices to a dish; they vary from cook to cook and can be hot, medium, mild, heavy with sauce or completely dry. *Dahi* (yogurt) is a frequently used ingredient. Two of the nation's outstanding dishes are chicken preparations, *tandoori murgha,* prepared with spices in a reddish sauce, and *morgee korma,* chicken and yogurt. Tea is unquestionably the national drink, and, interestingly, meals in India have no names—you are simply invited to dine at a certain hour. Tag it what you want by your own eating hours but don't pass up the invitation!

Curried Fish SERVES 6 *155 calories per serving*

1½ tablespoons butter or margarine
6 fillets of sole, flounder or haddock (4 ounces each)
2 onions, sliced

1 cup sliced celery
1 teaspoon salt
¼ teaspoon pepper
3 teaspoons curry powder†
¾ cup yogurt

Preheat oven to 350°.

Cut the fish into 1-inch strips. Grease a baking dish with 1 teaspoon butter; spread the fillets in it.

Melt the remaining butter in a skillet; sauté the onions and celery for 5 minutes. Stir in the salt, pepper, curry powder and yogurt. Pour over the fish. Bake 35 minutes.

† If a hotter flavor is desired, add chili peppers in addition to the curry powder.

Pickled Vegetables   SERVES 8 *about 25 calories per serving*

2 cucumbers
2 carrots
2 green peppers
8 small white onions
½ cup chopped onions
3 garlic cloves, minced
1½ teaspoons turmeric
½ teaspoon dried ground chili peppers

2 teaspoons powdered ginger
2 teaspoons salt
¼ cup ground almonds
2 tablespoons low calorie granulated sugar replacement*
3 cups white vinegar
1 cup water

Peel the cucumbers and carrots; slice thin. Cut the green peppers in ½-inch strips; quarter the onions lengthwise. Cover the vegetables with boiling water, let stand 1 minute, then drain.

Pound or chop together the chopped onions, garlic, turmeric, chili peppers, ginger, salt, almonds and sugar replacement. Combine with the vinegar and water and vegetables in a saucepan. Bring to a boil and cook 10 minutes; cool and let pickle 12-24 hours before serving. Keeps 2 weeks in the refrigerator.

* See page 5.

Indonesia

Rijstaffel is the world-renowned Indonesian rice table garnering a host of ingredients and spices and eaten almost *every day* by some Indonesians. Sound exotic and romantic—it's all that and delicious too. Indonesia? That's romantic too, particularly Java and Bali (part of the Republic also consisting of Borneo and Sumatra). *Rijstaffel,* to further explain, is a number of dishes served separately but eaten by each person in a large soup bowl filled with rice. Be careful! Some can be quite spicy. To temper the heat, *sambals,* an assortment of quieter relishes, or vegetable salads are served in accompaniment. Another favorite is *nasi goreng* (*nasi* meaning rice), which is a delightful concoction of chicken, shrimp and peanuts. Beer is the drink in Indonesia and often quite necessary to the fiery, exciting cuisine.

Indonesian Vegetable Salad   SERVES 8   *95 calories per serving*

2 tablespoons vegetable oil	½ cup milk
¼ cup finely chopped onions	¾ cup water
2 cloves garlic, minced	shredded lettuce
2 tablespoons peanut butter	1 cup cooked sliced green beans
1 teaspoon low calorie granulated sugar replacement*	1 cup shredded cabbage, cooked 5 minutes
½ teaspoon salt	2 tomatoes, diced
¼ teaspoon dried ground chili peppers	2 cucumbers, sliced
2 teaspoons grated lemon rind	2 hard-cooked eggs, coarsely chopped

Heat the oil in a skillet; sauté the onions and garlic 3 minutes. Stir in the peanut butter, sugar replacement, salt, chili peppers, lemon rind, and very gradually the milk mixed with the water. Cook over low heat 5 minutes, stirring frequently. Cool. This is the dressing.

Make a bed of the lettuce. Arrange the beans, cabbage, tomatoes and cucumbers over it. Sprinkle with the eggs. Serve the cooled dressing in a separate bowl.

* See page 5.

Iran

Glittering Persia, now Iran, has access to one of the most fabled foods known to man. Iranian caviar, from the Caspian Sea, is considered of the most superior quality. Much is exported, and even in Iran, caviar is quite expensive. But, to the more normal eating habits of Iranians, we find lamb and rice of prime importance, and *chelow kebab*, skewered lamb on rice, is truly the national dish. Fresh fruit and vegetables are abundant, and melons are so savored that gourmets keep them in storerooms to ripen slowly so they may be eaten at the precise moment of maturity and perfection. Eggplant is a favorite vegetable.

Iranian Eggplant Appetizer

MAKES ABOUT 3 CUPS
10 calories in 1 tablespoon

1 small eggplant
2 tablespoons olive or
   vegetable oil
1 cup chopped onions
2 green peppers, chopped
2 tablespoons tomato paste

1½ teaspoons salt
½ teaspoon freshly ground
   black pepper
1 teaspoon low calorie granulated sugar replacement*
1 tablespoon lemon juice

Peel and dice the eggplant. Heat the oil in a skillet; sauté the onions, eggplant and green peppers 20 minutes, stirring frequently. Stir in the tomato paste, salt, pepper and sugar replacement. Cook over low heat 10 minutes, mixing frequently. Add the lemon juice. Chill and serve with thin fingers of pumpernickel.

* See page 5.

Ireland

Green Ireland is a land of quiet charm and mystery. It takes digging to learn of its treasures, including its food treasures. Breakfast (the meal as a whole), appetizers, seafood and soups offer a wealth of Irish treats. Local fish—salmon, oysters and prawns are invariably fresh and delicious. Scallop soup, from the Aran Islands, sometimes made with clams, cockles or herring is outstanding. Pork products, bacon thick-and-sizzling to ham steak are cured beautifully. And Irish coffee?—all Ireland, to be sure, but invented at that famous-but-unlikely spot, Shannon Airport, itself. Shannon, take a bow.

Aran Scallop Soup   SERVES 8   *145 calories per serving*

1 pound scallops	3 cups bottled clam juice
2 slices bacon	3 cups water
1 tablespoon butter or margarine	1 teaspoon salt
1½ cups chopped onions	½ teaspoon freshly ground black pepper
1 leek, white part only, diced	½ teaspoon thyme
1 stalk celery, diced	6 sprigs parsley
1½ cups thinly sliced mushrooms	½ pound potatoes, peeled and diced
1 pound tomatoes, peeled and chopped	2 cups skim milk

Wash, drain and dice the scallops.

Dice the bacon, and brown it lightly in a saucepan. Pour off the fat, and add the butter or margarine, onions, leek, celery, mushrooms and tomatoes. Cook over low heat 5 minutes, stirring frequently. Add the clam juice, water, salt, pepper, thyme and parsley. Bring to a boil, and cook over low heat 30 minutes. Add the potatoes, cook 20 minutes. Add the scallops; cook 10 minutes. Discard the parsley and stir in the milk. Taste for seasoning. Heat, and serve.

Chicken, Family Style   SERVES 4   *230 calories per serving*

1 4-pound chicken,
   disjointed
1 tablespoon vegetable oil
2 tablespoons flour
4 cups water
10 small white onions
2 teaspoons salt
¼ teaspoon white pepper

3 sprigs parsley
1 bay leaf
12 mushroom caps, washed
   and dried
1 egg yolk
2 tablespoons milk
1 teaspoon lemon juice
   parsley sprigs

Wash and dry the chicken. Heat the oil in a heavy saucepan and stir in the flour. Add the water, stirring to the boiling point. Add the chicken, onions, salt, pepper, parsley and bay leaf. Cover and cook over medium heat 45 minutes. Add the mushrooms and cook 15 minutes longer.

Transfer chicken to a hot serving platter and surround with the onions and mushrooms. Strain the stock. Beat the egg yolk and milk in a bowl, add a little of the hot stock, stirring steadily to prevent curdling. Add to balance of stock and heat but do not let boil. Mix in the lemon juice and pour the sauce over chicken. Garnish with the parsley.

Israel

Israel is a nation of conflict. Sometimes quiet, other times violent, this conflict started many years ago and will probably reach a satisfactory compromise in the years to come. Being a land filled with so many Europeans who are bound to the traditional Jewish-European cooking habits, but presently situated in a warm climate inappropriate for heavy cooking—watch out—comes the clash! The answer is the elevation to importance of some of what might have been termed "summer cooking," elimination of the richer European recipes, and the acceptance of certain Arabic dishes suited to the climate. *Borscht* (cold beet soup), *schav* (soup made from sorrel grass, also cold), *gefilte fish* (stuffed fresh-water fish), chopped liver, *hallah* (egg bread) and *blintzes* (rolled pancakes with assorted fillings) remain important. *Falafel* (fried mashed chick-peas), of Arabic origin, is a great snack favorite, and fruits, salads and sherbets are gaining in popularity.

Chopped Chicken Livers   SERVES 6

105 calories per serving

1 pound chicken livers
2 cups chopped onions
¾ cup canned chicken broth
1 teaspoon salt

½ teaspoon freshly ground black pepper
dash nutmeg
1 tablespoon cognac

Wash the livers, removing any discolored spots. Cover with water, bring to a boil, and cook over low heat 5 minutes. Drain.

Combine the onions and ¼ cup broth in a saucepan. Bring to a boil and cook over medium heat until the liquid is absorbed, then add another ¼ cup broth and cook again until liquid is absorbed. Add the remaining broth and cook 5 minutes.

Put the livers, onions, salt, pepper and cognac in an electric-blender bowl and blend until smooth. If you don't have a blender, force the mixture through a food mill, or chop. Taste for seasoning. Chill and serve on lettuce leaves.

Fish, Israeli Style   SERVES 6   *110 calories per serving*

1 tablespoon vegetable oil	2 lemons, sliced thin
2 cups sliced onions	½ cup water
6 slices pike,	1 tablespoon cider vinegar
whitefish or mackerel	2 teaspoons low calorie
2 teaspoons salt	granulated
½ teaspoon pepper	sugar-replacement*
1½ cups tomatoes, diced	1 bay leaf

Heat the oil in a deep skillet. Brown the onions in it. Arrange the
fish over the onions and sprinkle with the salt and pepper. Add the
tomatoes, lemon slices, water, vinegar, sugar and bay leaf. Cover and
bake in a 325° oven 40 minutes, removing the cover for the last 5
minutes. Remove bay leaf. Serve hot or cold.

* See page 5.

Italy

Italians live life with joy and gusto. It's reflected in their cuisine, a marvelous mixture of the subtle and strong, peasant and patrician. Most commonly known in the United States as representational of Italian cooking is the southern type, rich in garlic, oils, spices and tomatoes. This is very unlike northern or even some central Italian cuisine, which is buttery and delicate. No other country of its size can boast of so many excellent region-to-region or, for that matter, city-to-city specialties. From the south, in Naples, pizza, of course, *zuppa di vongole* (clam soup) and *gelati* (ices). From Bologna, a marvelous assortment of pasta—noodles of all sizes, textures and shapes. Milan contributes many excellent rice dishes and the world-renowned *costoletta alla* Milanese, a lightly breaded veal chop. Venice offers an excellent variety of sea food; Rome many fine dishes including *fettuccine alla Romana,* a delicious concoction of noodles mixed with butter and cream cheese. So on and on, with a bewildering wealth of regional delicacies. And, with all this, *vino* stands supreme as the national drink. Much of the wine produced in Italy is of excellent quality. To finish the repast, espresso—strong, black coffee steamed in a gleaming espresso machine—is usually welcome and delicious.

Veal Cacciatore   SERVES 6   *255 calories per serving*

1½ pounds leg of veal, sliced ½ inch thick	1 tablespoon olive oil ¼ pound mushrooms, sliced
3 tablespoons flour	3 tablespoons chopped onion
1½ teaspoons salt	¼ cup dry white wine
¼ teaspoon pepper	½ cup canned tomatoes, drained

Have the butcher pound the veal very thin and cut into 12 pieces. Dredge the veal with a mixture of the flour, salt and pepper. Heat the oil in a skillet; sauté the veal over low heat until browned on both sides. Transfer to a serving dish and keep warm while preparing the sauce.

Cook the mushrooms and onions for 5 minutes in the oil remaining in the skillet. Add the wine and tomatoes. Cook over medium heat 5 minutes. Correct the seasoning, pour over the veal and serve.

Green Rice   SERVES 6   *145 calories per serving*

1 tablespoon butter or margarine	2 carrots, grated 1 cup raw rice
1 cup chopped raw spinach	3 cups canned chicken broth
4 green onions, chopped	1½ teaspoons salt
½ cup chopped parsley	¼ teaspoon pepper

Melt the butter in a casserole; sauté the spinach, onions, parsley and carrots for 10 minutes, stirring frequently. Add the rice and stir until it is well coated with the vegetable mixture. Add the broth, salt and pepper. Cover and cook over low heat 30 minutes or until rice is tender.

Japan

To the Japanese, the beauty of their food is as important as the taste of it. Some of the most uncomplicated dishes in their national repertoire taste so appetizing because they simply look so good! Since the Japanese cook almost completely without dairy fats the cuisine provides excellent diet fare. In addition to rice, fish and other seafoods are the backbone of the Japanese table. Certain special cooking ingredients give Japanese food its distinctive qualities. Among these are *shoyu* (soy sauce) which is quite salty and eliminates the use of ordinary table salt, *miso,* a paste made from fermented soybeans and salt, *tōfu* (bean curd), and *ajimomoto,* monosodium glutamate. Interesting dishes include *sukiyaki* and *tempura;* the former being open pan-fried beef slices with vegetables; the latter deep-fried batter-encased foods. *Sushi* restaurants are to be found throughout Japan; these serve a thin slice of raw fish wrapped around a small quantity of boiled rice sprinkled with a choice of seasonings. It may sound too difficult for the ordinary palate to bear, but the Japanese use the freshest of fish, and the end result is quite appetizing. *Sake,* a rice wine (served warm) and tea are the national drinks, but coffee is becoming a great favorite.

Sukiyaki   SERVES 6   *405 calories per serving*

1 tablespoon peanut or
  vegetable oil
1½ pounds sirloin steak, ¼ inch
  thick, cut into strips
  ½ inch × 2 inches
½ cup soy sauce
2 tablespoons low calorie granulated sugar replacement*
1 tablespoon sherry
½ cup beef broth

3 onions, sliced thin
1 cup sliced celery
1 cup sliced bamboo shoots
½ pound mushrooms,
  sliced thin
4 scallions (green onions),
  sliced
½ pound fresh spinach
  (washed thoroughly
  and drained)

Heat the oil in a large skillet (if you want to prepare the dish at the table, use an electric frying pan or chafing dish). Brown the meat over high heat, then push it to one side. Combine the soy sauce, sugar replacement, sherry and broth. Pour half the mixture over the meat.

Cook the onions and celery in the skillet for 3 minutes, then push them to one side and add the remaining soy-sauce mixture, bamboo shoots, mushrooms, scallions, and spinach. Cook 4 minutes. Don't overcook, as everything should be crisp.

Serve directly from the skillet with ¼ cup of rice for each serving.
* See page 5.

Malaysia

Like other Asiatic countries with warm climates, Malaysians prefer highly spiced dishes. Probably the only simple food is the basic boiled rice. After that we're definitely in spice country! Beside the usual seasonings, you find, to name a few, lemon grass *(serai),* mustard seeds *(sawi),* tamarind *(asam),* candlenuts *(nuah keras),* fenugreek *(ventayam),* and poppy seeds *(kaskas).* The lush countryside provides a wealth of fruits and vegetables all very popular in the diet. Among the meat dishes are *kurma* (beef or mutton flavored with cinnamon, cloves, white pepper, garlic and onions), *rendan santan* (a coconut-ginger chicken dish), and *dondeng* (spicy bits of steak with tamarind, garlic, onions and ginger). It's all quite exotic, and if your taste buds like that flavor, Malaysia is a gourmet Bali Ha'i. Banana desserts are a favorite, a cooling end to a spicy meal.

Bananas In Coconut   SERVES 6   *95 calories per serving*

3 firm bananas
1 tablespoon butter or
   margarine
1 teaspoon cornstarch
¼ cup orange juice

2 tablespoons low calorie
   granulated sugar
   replacement*
1 tablespoon brown sugar
¼ cup shredded coconut

Preheat oven to 375°.

Peel the bananas; cut in half crosswise, then lengthwise. Grease a shallow baking dish. Arrange bananas in it. Mix the cornstarch, orange juice and sugar replacement until smooth. Pour mixture over the bananas. Sprinkle with the brown sugar and coconut.

Bake 15 minutes or until easily pierced with a fork. Serve warm.

* See page 5.

Mexico

The language may be Spanish but the food is practically pure Mexican, as the Indian heritage shows up strongly in the cuisine. Corn is the staple food and *pulque* (from the maguey cactus plant) the national drink. From corn comes the *tortilla*. *Tortillas* are like bread. When fried they are *tostados;* when filled with beans or meats they are *tacos*. One of the high points of the cuisine is *mole de guajolote* (turkey in mole sauce) which includes, among other ingredients, chocolate. Before you reject the thought, taste. Delicious!

Eggs Ranch Style   SERVES 6   *110 calories per serving*

1 tablespoon butter or margarine	1 teaspoon salt
2 onions, sliced thin	1 teaspoon chili powder
3 tomatoes, peeled and diced	⅛ teaspoon freshly ground black pepper
2 green peppers, diced	½ cup water
	6 eggs

Melt the butter in a skillet (use one you can serve from if you have it). Sauté the onions until lightly browned. Add the tomatoes and green peppers; cook 5 minutes. Stir in the salt, chili powder, pepper and water. Cook 10 minutes.

Carefully break the eggs over the vegetable mixture. Bake in a 350° oven 10 minutes, or until the eggs are set.

Morocco

"My life for a spoon" flashed through the mind of a dazed visitor to Morocco being served *couscous* for dinner without a utensil in sight. This can and does happen in Morocco when dining at a home or restaurant not included on the traditional tourist route. To further explain, *couscous* is a cereal-type dish made from bits of *faufal* (wheat), steamed with lamb or mutton and spices to form a marvelous concoction much favored by natives of North Africa. Delicious but difficult without a spoon! Moroccan eating habits still favor the right hand (with only an occasional assist from the left) over utensils. Spices like pepper, cinnamon, and chervil, are Moroccan favorites. Minted tea in the middle of a repast is used in order to refresh the palate. Vegetables never appear as plain vegetables, but rather like the vegetable pie that follows.

Vegetable Pie   SERVES 6   75 *calories per serving*

1 pound fresh spinach, chopped, or 1 package frozen chopped, thawed	1½ teaspoons salt
	¼ teaspoon freshly ground black pepper
2½ cups chopped green onions	2 tablespoons chopped walnuts
1 cup chopped lettuce	3 eggs, beaten
1½ cups chopped parsley	2 tablespoons butter or margarine
2 tablespoons flour	

Wash the fresh spinach, drain well and chop. Or drain the thawed frozen chopped spinach. Mix together the spinach, green onions, lettuce, parsley, flour, salt, pepper and nuts. Mix in the eggs.

Melt the butter in an 11-inch pieplate. Pour the vegetable mixture into it. Bake in a preheated 325° oven 1 hour or until top is brown and crisp.

Netherlands

Food is a very serious matter in the Netherlands. It's a country that loves to eat—sometimes six times a day! Breakfast is large, usually including hot cereal made from groats. Coffee and cake follow at eleven. By one, it's lunchtime; 4:30 P.M. brings small sandwiches and little cakes for energy. Dinner is early, and before retiring, cocoa and cold meats, or leftover cake, fit the bill. It's really no place to keep a diet going, but among the favored dishes are a few that aren't overly calorific—mostly the lovely fish and seafood: herring, shrimp, lobster, eel, mussels and the famous Zeeland oysters. Chicken is also a favorite, often baked in different ways. *Lofschotel* (baked endive wrapped in ham) would please without doing too much harm to the figure, but the favorite soup, *ertwensoep,* and the national drink, beer, aren't exactly low on the calorie chart.

Stuffed Breast of Veal

300 calories per serving†

1 breast of veal
1 tablespoon butter or
    margarine
2 onions, minced
½ pound mushrooms, sliced
1 cup shredded cabbage
1 slice white bread,
    trimmed and cubed
3 gherkins, diced
3 teaspoons salt
½ teaspoon freshly ground
    black pepper
1 teaspoon paprika
½ cup canned beef broth

Have a pocket made in the veal breast for stuffing. Melt the butter in a skillet, add the onions, mushrooms, and cabbage and sauté 10 minutes. Mix in the bread cubes, gherkins, 1 teaspoon salt and ¼ teaspoon pepper. Mix the remaining salt and pepper with the paprika and rub into the veal. Fill the pocket with the sautéed stuffing and close the opening with skewers, thread or toothpicks.

Put veal in a roasting pan and roast in a 375° oven for 30 minutes. Reduce the heat to 350°, add the beef broth and roast 2 hours longer or until tender, basting frequently and adding a little water if the pan becomes dry. For each serving, allow 2 ribs and 4 tablespoons stuffing. becomes dry.

† For each serving, allow 2 ribs and 4 tablespoons stuffing.

Baked Breast of Chicken   SERVES 6   *175 calories per serving*

3 whole chicken breasts
2 tablespoons flour
2 teaspoons salt
½ teaspoon freshly ground
    black pepper
2 tablespoons butter or
    margarine
1 clove garlic, minced
¼ cup diced ham

½ pound mushrooms,
    chopped
½ cup shelled green peas
1 stalk celery
2 sprigs parsley
1 bay leaf
1 cup dry white wine
1 head lettuce, cut in
    6 wedges

Cut the breasts in half through the breast bone. Wash and dry.

Mix the flour, salt and pepper. Rub the chicken with the seasoned flour.

Melt the butter in a casserole, add the chicken breasts and garlic. Brown lightly on both sides. Cover the chicken breasts with the ham, mushrooms and peas. Add the celery, parsley, bay leaf and wine to the casserole and place the lettuce wedges over all. Bake in a 350° oven for 1 hour or until chicken is tender.

New Zealand

The general food patterns and customs of New Zealand follow very closely those of Australia, which follow closely those of England. In New Zealand, however, the native Maoris have had some influence on introducing local foodstuffs into the everyday diet of the European New Zealanders, and some of the reverse is also true. The local waters provide excellent fish and seafood, including a unique green clam called the *toheroa,* a rare shellfish called the *pipi,* and *paupas,* an abalone-like shellfish. An interesting specialty is the "half-bird, half-fish" mutton bird which nests along the sea and lives exclusively on fish, this distinctly flavoring its own taste. The meat of this bird is quite oily and the water in which it is cooked has to be changed at least three times to make it palatable. Interesting vegetables abound and salads are well prepared. Desserts are usually family recipes brought from England, such as the lemon pudding. Tea is the national beverage, and tea time a definite custom, but as in many other countries, coffee is becoming more popular.

Lemon Pudding   SERVES 6   *110 calories per serving*

4 tablespoons cornstarch	3 tablespoons nonfat dry milk
¼ teaspoon salt	½ cup low calorie
3 eggs, separated	granulated sugar
⅓ cup lemon juice	replacement*
1½ cups skim milk	1 tablespoon melted butter

Preheat oven to 350°.

Sift the cornstarch and salt into a bowl. Add the egg yolks and lemon juice, beating until smooth. Gradually add the skim milk and dry milk. Beat again.

Beat the egg whites until stiff but not dry. Beat in the sugar replacement. Fold the lemon mixture into the egg whites. Melt the butter in a 1½-quart casserole or baking dish. Turn the lemon mixture into the baking dish. Place in a shallow pan of hot water.

Bake 55 minutes, or until set and browned. Remove from oven and let cool in the pan of water.

* See page 5.

Norway

The land of the breathtaking fjords brings us some very unusual dishes. Particularly *sildegryn* and *rensdyrstek*—that's herring soup and reindeer steak respectively! And respectfully. Both are quite good, as is much of the cuisine of this country. Fish is everywhere. A Norwegian housewife often shops for her dinner directly from the boat of her favorite fisherman. Next in popularity is game—all sorts, like elk, bear and grouse. Bear hard to bear? Not so different as you might expect. Less exotic are the excellent fresh dairy products including cheeses, some of which are of the highest caliber in Scandinavia.

Fish Pudding   SERVES 6   *225 calories per serving*

2 tablespoons butter or margarine
1½ cups sliced onions
2 cups thinly sliced potatoes
3 cups cooked or canned flaked fish (herring or cod)
½ teaspoon pepper
2 teaspoons salt
2 eggs
1½ cups milk

Melt 1 tablespoon butter in a skillet. Brown the onions in it. Butter a baking dish with remaining butter. Arrange alternate layers of the potatoes, fish and onions in the baking dish, starting and ending with the potatoes. Sprinkle each layer with pepper and salt (using 1½ teaspoons of salt).

Beat the eggs, milk and ½ teaspoon salt together and pour over the top layer.

Bake in a 350° oven 45 minutes or until browned and set.

Pakistan

It is only natural that Pakistan, once part of India, should have a similar cuisine. All the basic foodstuffs are very much the same, with certain interesting Pakistani variations. *Pulaos* (spiced rice dishes) are major favorites, and some of them are very hot. Fish (though not too plentiful) is held in high esteem particularly in a dish called *beckti Kashmiri,* prepared with garlic and chili peppers. Lamb is the most popular meat, and in the fowl family chicken dishes rate high and are prepared quite well. *Chicken Tikka,* a spiced chicken, is tasty and regarded favorably by the neighboring Middle Eastern countries. Sweet fruit drinks, milk, buttermilk and tea are the favored beverages.

Chicken Tikka   SERVES 4   *250 calories per serving*

2 cups yogurt	2 teaspoons ground
¼ cup lemon juice	coriander
2 teaspoons salt	¼ teaspoon anise
½ teaspoon dried ground	2 broilers (1¼ pounds each)
chili peppers	2 tablespoons vegetable oil

Mix together the yogurt, lemon juice, salt, chili peppers, coriander and anise. The broilers can be left whole, split, or quartered. Marinate the chicken in the sauce for at least 24 hours—48 is even better. Drain well, brush with oil and roast, either in a rotisserie, in a 375° oven, or over charcoal. The time will vary depending on whether the chicken is whole, split, or quartered.

Peru

Peru offers vivid contrasts geographically. The same applies to its cuisine. A great favorite is a simple *seviche*—raw fish pickled in such a way that it tastes cooked. It is not as hard to eat as it may sound. Another national snack is *anticuchos,* pieces of beef heart or liver dipped in a spicy sauce and roasted over a charcoal fire. In contrast to these, partridges and other game birds are prepared in delicate sauces. Fruits are excellent and eaten often, and the juicy, green *cherimoya,* locally cultivated, has an exquisite flavor. This country boasts some very unusual drinks. *Pisco* (a grape brandy) is used to concoct a *"pisco* sour" Peru's favorite mixed drink, which has, among its ingredients, honey and egg white.

Chicken Liver Anticuchos   SERVES 6   *165 calories per serving*

24 mushroom caps	½ teaspoon salt
18 chicken livers	½ teaspoon tabasco
6 slices bacon, half-cooked and cut in thirds	1 tablespoon vegetable oil
	6 tablespoons chili sauce

You'll need 6 skewers for this dish. Sprinkle the livers and mushrooms with salt, tabasco and oil. Arrange the mushrooms, livers and bacon on the skewers, starting and ending with the mushrooms.

Place skewers on a rack and broil in a hot broiler, turning them frequently, until ingredients are browned.

Heat the chili sauce and serve with the brochettes.

Philippines

At a formal dinner party in the Philippines there's an unusual custom. The hostess does not participate in the meal with the guests, but stands near the head of the table overseeing the service and watching to see if the guests have all they need. During the evening you're sure to be served at least one of these delicious specialties: *escabeche* (pickled spicy fish), *morcón* (stuffed meat roll), tomatoes stuffed with shrimp, *lechón* (whole barbecued pig), and much delicious local beer. When you wake up next morning, don't expect the usual little hot-weather-country breakfast. A surprisingly heavy breakfast is served, but you can always swap the hot chocolate for coffee.

Baked Shrimp-Stuffed Tomatoes   SERVES 6

175 calories per serving

6 large tomatoes (of equal size)
2 tablespoons vegetable oil
½ cup chopped onions
1 pound raw shrimp, shelled, deveined and chopped
1½ teaspoons salt
½ teaspoon freshly ground black pepper
½ cup dry bread crumbs
¼ cup milk

Buy firm tomatoes. Cut a ½-inch piece crosswise from the stem end and reserve. Carefully scoop out the pulp and reserve. Heat 1 tablespoon oil in a skillet; sauté the onions 5 minutes. Add the tomato pulp. Cook over low heat 5 minutes. Stir the shrimp, salt and pepper into the mixture; cook over low heat 5 minutes. Mix in the bread crumbs and milk; stuff the tomatoes and cover with the tops.

Oil a baking pan with 1 tablespoon of oil. Arrange the stuffed tomatoes in the pan. Bake in a 375° oven 20 minutes or until tomatoes are tender.

Poland

Poland was once part of Russia, and its cuisine (and climate) are quite similar. There are certain subtle differences. In Russia they spell vodka *that* way and in Poland it's *woudka*—differences like that. A favorite here is *borscht* (beef and cabbage soup), actually, in Polish, *barszcz*. Seasonings and ingredients vary a bit from the Russian. Stews like *Bigos* are very popular. The Polish people are quite fond of field-growing vegetables like cucumbers, radishes and scallions, and prepare them many different ways. Also a national favorite is the mushroom, which finds its way into almost every dish, as well as outside the country for profitable export. Tea and coffee, when one can afford them, are the national drink favorites.

Bigos   SERVES 6

430 calories per serving

2 tablespoons butter or
  margarine
5 onions, chopped
2 tablespoons paprika
2 pounds beef (chuck or cross
  rib) cut in 1½-inch cubes

2 teaspoons salt
½ teaspoon pepper
1 8-ounce can tomato sauce
4 tablespoons yogurt

Melt the butter in a Dutch oven or heavy saucepan; sauté the onions over very low heat until soft, stirring frequently. Sprinkle with the paprika, and add the beef. Brown the beef on all sides, then add the salt, pepper and tomato sauce. Cover and cook over low heat 2 hours, or until meat is tender.

Skim off the fat and taste for seasoning. Stir in the yogurt and serve.

Portugal

Visit Portugal and it seems the whole country is fishing. The docks are alive with the sea—it's quite a sight. Naturally, the cuisine follows the catch. Oysters and crabs are absolutely delicious and prepared countless different ways. Soups and chowders follow. The sardine is exported canned, but preferred here at home either fresh or dried. This excellent table doesn't end with the sea—there are outstanding meat dishes, two of the most noteworthy being *iscas* (calf's liver) and *carne de vinha* (spicy pickled meat). Local fruits are superb, and for dessert enjoy Portuguese cheese—some of these absolutely first-class, particularly the ones made from ewe's milk.

Calf's Liver In Wine Sauce   SERVES 4   *235 calories per serving*

2 cloves garlic, minced
1 bay leaf
1 teaspoon salt
½ teaspoon pepper
¼ cup dry white wine
1 pound thinly sliced
    calf's liver
2 tablespoons vegetable oil

In a bowl combine the garlic, bay leaf, salt, pepper and wine. Add the liver and marinate in the refrigerator overnight, turning occasionally.

Heat the oil in a skillet until it smokes. Carefully add the liver and marinade and cook over medium heat 5 minutes, stirring gently but constantly. Serve at once.

Noodles With Tuna Sauce   SERVES 6   *130 calories per serving*

1 tablespoon olive oil	¼ teaspoon freshly ground
2 cloves garlic, minced	black pepper
½ pound mushrooms,	¼ teaspoon basil
sliced	1 can (7 ounces) tuna fish
1 cup canned tomato	3 tablespoons chopped
sauce	parsley
1 cup water	1 pound broad noodles,
1 teaspoon salt	cooked and drained

Heat the oil in a saucepan; sauté the garlic and mushrooms 5 minutes.
Add the tomato sauce, water, salt, pepper and basil. Cover and cook
over low heat 45 minutes. Drain the tuna, wash under cold running
water and drain again. Flake it and add to the sauce with the parsley.
Cook 10 minutes. Taste for seasoning and serve over the noodles.

Puerto Rico

Corn, sweet potatoes, mani, (peanuts), cassava, yautia and leren (roots of unusual flavor), were all first found in Puerto Rico. The explorers introduced Spanish cooking to the natives and the 20th century result is a pure mixture of Spain-and-Puerto Rico. Being an island, it is only natural that fish should play an important part in Puerto Rico's cookery. Snapper, lobster, crabs, mullet, mackerel and pompano abound. Then the Spanish influence comes into play with *paella* and *gazpacho* (see Spain). Chicken is the prime poultry, and dishes like *arroz con pollo* (a direct Spanish descendant), and *asopao* "soupy rice" (pure Puerto Rican) is made with chicken, ham, pimentos and vegetables, and a great island favorite. Flan (custard) is an import from Spain, but other desserts are assorted fruits, all grown in Puerto Rico, and delicious!

Fish Stew   SERVES 6   *185 calories per serving*

1 lobster (1 pound)
1 tablespoon olive oil
2 onions, chopped
2 cloves garlic, minced
1 pound haddock or cod, cubed
3 tablespoons uncooked rice
2 potatoes, peeled and cubed

2 cups coarsely shredded cabbage
1 cup canned tomatoes
2 tablespoons tomato paste
5 cups water
2 teaspoons salt
½ teaspoon pepper
½ teaspoon oregano

Have the fish man split the uncooked lobster for you—then it will be a simple process to remove the meat and cut it into pieces. Don't forget the claw meat, too. Reserve the shells, as it will help to flavor the stew.

Heat the olive oil in a deep saucepan; sauté the onions and garlic for 5 minutes. Add the fish, lobster and rice; cook over high heat for 5 minutes, stirring almost constantly. Add the potatoes, cabbage, tomatoes, tomato paste, water, salt, pepper, oregano and some of the lobster shells. Cook over medium heat 20 minutes. Taste for seasoning, discard the lobster shells and serve in deep bowls.

This is a complete dish—soup, fish and vegetables all in one.

Rumania

Rumanians develop cults about their food. When they like something it's everywhere—every meal, every restaurant, every home. Into this category fall three items in particular: *mamaliga* (a boiled-then-baked cornmeal dish), replacing bread as the national starch, *ikra* (Russian caviar), which is beloved but a bit too expensive for every meal, and *tchorbas* (many different types of sour soups based on fermentation agents like lemon, vine leaves or sauerkraut). *Ghivetch*, a medley of fresh, well-prepared vegetables, is usually served with *mamaliga*. *Urda* and *branza de burdf* are outstanding local cheeses incorporated often into Rumanian meals. Chicken is a luxury, and is served on special occasions in imaginative ways such as with chestnuts.

Chicken-Chestnut Stew   SERVES 6   *200 calories per serving*

2 tablespoons butter or margarine
1 5-pound fowl, disjointed
2 onions, chopped
2½ teaspoons salt
1 teaspoon paprika
2 tablespoons tomato paste
1½ cups water
½ pound uncooked chestnuts, peeled

Melt the butter in a heavy saucepan; sauté the chicken until brown on all sides. Stir in the onions; cover and cook until onions brown. Stir occasionally. Add the salt, paprika, tomato paste and water. Cover and cook over low heat 1 hour. Add the chestnuts, cover, and cook 1 hour longer or until chicken and chestnuts are tender. Watch carefully and add a little water if necessary.

Russia

So few foodstuffs except the most commonplace reach the Russian marketplace. However, on state occasions, some of the old delicacies appear again, and then the glories of Russian cuisine are remembered with delight. It all used to start with the lovely custom of *zakouski,* meaning appetizers. Prominent among these were caviar, salmon and herring (all accompanied by vodka, of course) laid out *smörgasbord* style. Soups were next, and very important, Russian winters being what they are. *Borscht,* the base made from beets or cabbage, with many ingredients varying from house to house, and *schtchi,* an excellent sauerkraut soup, were two of the most popular. Meats, particularly lamb, were prepared *shashlik* style, marinated and grilled on a skewer. Bitoks are extremely popular. Chicken was treated very well, two of the most popular classics being *cotleki Pojarski* (ground and formed into a cutlet), and *chicken Kiev* (boned breast of chicken wrapped around a nugget of butter). Tea, the national drink, is always made with leaves, and there is the Russian claim that if the water is first boiled in a samovar the flavor is unexcelled.

Bitoks SERVES 6   *205 calories per serving*

1 pound lean top round,
    ground
1 slice white bread, trimmed
¼ cup skim milk
2 teaspoons grated lemon rind
2 teaspoons minced parsley

1 teaspoon salt
¼ teaspoon freshly ground
    black pepper
1 egg white
3 tablespoons flour
2 tablespoons vegetable oil

Be sure all the fat is trimmed from the meat before it is ground. Soak the bread in the milk, drain and mash smooth. Mix together the meat, bread, lemon rind, parsley, salt, pepper and egg white. Sprinkle the flour onto a board and form the meat mixture into 1-inch round cakes, ½ inch thick.

Heat the oil in a skillet and brown the cakes in it 2 minutes on each side, or to desired degree of rareness.

Spain

Spain abounds with colorful dishes—pink shrimps, red tomatoes, green peppers, black olives, golden saffron rice. Tastes are dramatic too, and rarely spicy. Custom nods to a small breakfast followed by a large lunch and a late dinner, eaten after the heat of the day has fully subsided. *Paella Valenciana*, probably the most well-known of Spanish dishes, is a delicious combination of chicken, rice, lobster and shrimp. Chicken and rice, *Arroz con Pollo*, is a simple version. *Angulas* (baby eels) may sound exotic, but not after a taste or two. *Zarzuela de mariscos* (lovely sound, tastes the same, and literally translated means "a musical comedy of seafood") blends together a medley of local Spanish seafood. Another specialty, *gazpacho* (cold soup with a tomato base), is often called "salad-soup" because it incorporates a mélange of vegetables. Quite a treat on a hot day! Spanish sherry is world renowned; this and the food make for a most noteworthy cuisine.

Gazpacho SERVES 6 *70 calories per serving*

2 onions, chopped
2 cloves garlic, minced
3 green peppers, chopped
5 tomatoes, chopped
2 teaspoons salt
½ teaspoon freshly ground black pepper
2 teaspoons Spanish paprika
2 tablespoons olive or vegetable oil
⅓ cup wine vinegar
1½ cups water
1 cucumber, peeled and sliced thin

Combine the onions, garlic, green peppers, tomatoes, salt, pepper and paprika; purée in an electric blender or force through a sieve. Gradually stir in the oil, vinegar and water.

Chill in a bowl (non-metal) for 2 hours. Add the cucumbers just before serving. Croutons flavored with garlic may be served separately, if desired.

Chicken and Rice SERVES 6 *275 calories per serving*

1 3½-pound fryer, disjointed
3 tablespoons flour
2 teaspoons salt
2 tablespoons olive oil
2 onions, chopped
2 cloves garlic, minced
3 tomatoes, chopped
2 cups chicken broth,
    fresh or canned

1 bay leaf
½ teaspoon saffron
½ teaspoon pepper
1 cup uncooked rice
1 green pepper, diced
1 pimento, sliced
3 tablespoons sherry

Wash and dry the chicken. Mix the flour and salt together and roll the chicken in the mixture.

Heat the oil in a deep skillet or casserole. Sauté the onions and garlic for 10 minutes. Remove and brown the chicken in the oil remaining in the skillet. Return the onions, and add the tomatoes, broth, bay leaf, saffron and pepper. Cover and cook over low heat 30 minutes. Add the rice, green pepper, pimento and sherry. Cover and cook 30 minutes longer, or until chicken and rice are tender. Watch carefully to avoid burning and add a little more broth if necessary.

Sweden

Home of the smörgåsbord—what it tastes like in Sweden cannot be imitated. Sometimes fifty or more dishes. Basic rule: fish first, cold second, hot third. Simplified versions, where a one-plate smörgåsbord will do the trick, are, however, appearing on the scene. Some interesting dishes in or away from the smörgåsbord include *sillsallad* (herring with apples and beets), *fiskbullar* (delicious fish balls) *köttbullar* (the famous Swedish meatballs) and *sjömansbiff* (beef stew with beer). Everyone is familiar with Swedish pancakes, the national dessert.

Swedish Herring Salad   SERVES 8   *190 calories per serving*

2 salt-herrings fillets
  (Iceland, if available)
2 apples, peeled and diced
2 potatoes,
  cooked and diced
1 cup pickled beets, diced

⅓ cup onoins, diced
2 tablespoons low calorie
  granulated
  sugar replacement*
¼ teaspoon white pepper
½ cup cider vinegar

Soak the herring overnight, in water to cover. Drain well and dice. Add the apples, potatoes, beets and onions. Mix well. Blend together the sugar, pepper and vinegar. Add to the mixture and toss lightly. Chill. Garnish with chopped hard-cooked eggs and sour cream. Serve as a first course.

* See page 5.

Delicate Pancakes   SERVES 8   *25 calories per serving*

1 egg yolk
1½ cups skim milk
¼ teaspoon salt
1 tablespoon low calorie
   granulated sugar
   replacement*

½ cup sifted flour
1 egg white
2 tablespoons butter or
   margarine

Beat the egg yolk, milk, salt and sugar replacement. Add the flour, beating until smooth. Chill 2 hours.

Beat the egg white until stiff but not dry and fold it into the batter thoroughly. Melt 2 teaspoons butter (or margarine) in a skillet, griddle or Swedish pancake pan. Drop the batter by the tablespoonful and bake until lightly browned on both sides. Add fat as necessary.

* See page 5.

Switzerland

The freshness of the air in Switzerland seems to envelop its cuisine. Everywhere you go, from the simplest café to the most elaborate restaurant, from the dining cars on trains to the homes of its people, the food reflects the high standards of the country. Three languages are spoken in Switzerland: German, French and Italian—and the food is directly influenced by those countries. For a purely Swiss meal one would have to go to a family restaurant or be invited to dine in a home. The famous *fondue,* a bubbling pot of grated cheese eaten with fork-pronged pieces of bread, or the *fondue bourguignonne,* where the meat slices are dipped into hot oil and cooked piece by piece, are probably the most popular, typically Swiss dishes. Sausages of all types are in great demand, and many interesting varieties can be found throughout the countryside. Of course, cheese and chocolate are excellent, and Swiss brands are exported and known the world over.

Swiss Chocolate Dessert   SERVES 6

95 calories per serving

2 squares (ounces) unsweetened chocolate	3 egg yolks, beaten
⅔ cup low calorie granulated sugar replacement*	3 egg whites, stiffly beaten
	dash salt
	1 tablespoon cognac

Break the chocolate into small pieces and let it melt over hot water. Add the sugar replacement, egg yolks, salt and cognac, stirring constantly. Remove from the heat and immediately fold in the egg whites. Turn into 6 individual serving glasses. Chill for at least 5 hours. Serve with 1 tablespoon of low calorie whipped topping for each glass (see page 27).

* See page 5.

Thailand

Order a salad in Thailand and it's apt to come with ingredients you'd put in your company centerpiece. Made with rose petals, *khachorn* flowers and other exotic ingredients, it's a delightful taste treat hard to duplicate exactly, without a strain on the pocketbook. The rest of the cuisine shows definite Chinese and Indian influences, with rice the mainstay of the diet and *arak* (made from palm sap or rice) the favorite drink. A century ago the Siamese ate only a midday meal and another in the late evening. After the turn of the century a 3 P.M. refreshment (called *kruang wag*) became popular. This has become afternoon tea. Now breakfast is gaining favor. In the countryside, however, the old ways cling, and it's two meals a day—with much nibbling in between.

Sweet and Pungent Squabs   SERVES 6   *130 calories per serving*

3 squabs, rock cornish hens, or small broilers, split
1½ teaspoons salt
1 teaspoon minced garlic
1 tablespoon peanut oil
1 tablespoon cornstarch
3 tablespoons low calorie granulated sugar replacement*

½ cup vinegar
½ cup water
2 tablespoons soy sauce
½ teaspoon pepper
2 onions, sliced thin
2 green peppers, diced
3 tomatoes, cut in eighths
6 coriander seeds

Wash and dry the birds; sprinkle with the salt and garlic. Grease a baking pan with the oil and arrange the birds in it. Broil in a hot broiler 10 minutes on each side, or until birds are tender. While they are broiling, prepare the sauce.

In a saucepan, mix the cornstarch, sugar replacement, and vinegar until smooth. Cook over low heat, stirring constantly, until mixture reaches the boiling point. Add the water. Stir in the soy sauce, pepper, onions, green peppers, tomatoes and coriander seeds. Cook over low heat 10 minutes. Pour over the birds and serve.

* See page 5.

Turkey

Turkey loves its food—so much so that a gourmet here is regarded with reverence and homage accorded his opinions. Eating is an important matter and dinner almost always begins with soup. *Düğün chorbasi,* the traditional Turkish wedding soup, is classic, made with lamb, eggs, and a great deal of care. Fish is held in equal esteem, particularly swordfish, sturgeon, caviar and *hamsi,* a local cross between a sprat and an anchovy. *Kinch shiste* (marinated swordfish on skewers) is a fish recipe similar to the usual way of preparing lamb—that is, of course, *shish kebab.* A Middle East battle rages as to where *shish kebab* originated, but since the words are Turkish, the credit probably rests right here.

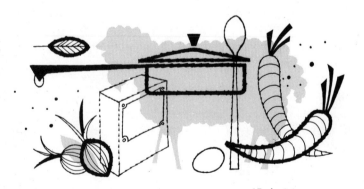

Lamb Pilau   SERVES 6   *305 calories per serving*

6 shoulder lamb chops	2 stalks celery, sliced
2 onions, chopped	3 cups boiling water
2 teaspoons salt	¾ cup uncooked rice
½ teaspoon pepper	¼ pound mushrooms,
1 bay leaf	chopped
2 carrots, sliced	1 egg yolk, beaten

Trim as much fat as possible from the chops. Brown on both sides in a skillet; pour off the fat. Add the onions and continue browning. Add the salt, pepper, bay leaf, carrots, celery, and 1½ cups boiling water. Cover and cook over low heat 40 minutes.

While the lamb is cooking, prepare the rice. Add the rice and mushrooms to the remaining boiling water. Cover and cook over low heat 20 minutes. Place in a casserole and add the sauce and the vegetables from the lamb. Stir in the egg yolk and taste for seasoning; arrange the chops on top.

Bake in a 375° oven 10 minutes. Serve directly from the casserole.

Union of South Africa

Practically the only possibility of tasting a true South African dinner is to be invited to an *Afrikaner* home. Hotels, restaurants and other tourist eating spots serve a strictly "international" menu that rarely features dishes evolving from the country itself. *Babottee,* a meat pie, and *bredec,* a stew, are typical favorites among the South African dishes. The country is comprised of four groups: natives (Bantu), Dutch, English and Indians. Each of these has their own distinct customs and eating habits. Food resources include the extraordinary rock lobster tail which is exported internationally (but tastes even better there) and a wonderful variety of exotic fruits and berries.

African Ground Beef   SERVES 6   *370 calories per serving*

1 tablespoon butter or margarine	2 eggs
2 onions, chopped	1 tablespoon curry powder
1 slice white bread, crumbled	1 teaspoon salt
½ cup skim milk	1 tablespoon lemon juice
1¼ pounds ground lean beef	2 tablespoons ground almonds

Melt the butter in a skillet; sauté the onions 10 minutes, stirring frequently.

Soak the bread in the milk, then squeeze dry, reserving the milk. Combine the bread with the beef, sautéed onions, 1 egg, the curry powder, salt, lemon juice and almonds. Mix well.

Pat the meat into a 9-inch pie plate. Beat the remaining egg with the reserved milk and pour over the meat.

Bake in a 350° oven 1 hour. Serve directly from the pie plate.

Curried Salmon   SERVES 6   *160 calories per serving*

2 pounds salmon	⅛ teaspoon dried ground
2 teaspoons salt	red pepper
½ teaspoon pepper	4 tablespoons seedless raisins
1 tablespoon vegetable or	3 tablespoons low calorie
olive oil	granulated sugar
3 onions, sliced thin	replacement*
1½ tablespoons curry powder	2 cups white vinegar

Have the salmon sliced thin and divide it into 6 pieces. Sprinkle the salt and pepper on the fish.

Heat the oil in a skillet; brown the salmon on both sides. Carefully remove; add one of the sliced onions to the oil in the skillet and sauté until browned.

In a saucepan combine the curry powder, red peppers, raisins, sugar replacement and vinegar; bring to a boil and cook over low heat 10 minutes.

Arrange the fish, sautéed onions and raw onions in layers in a glass bowl or jar. Pour the vinegar mixture over it. Cover and refrigerate for 48 hours before serving.

The salmon prepared in this manner keeps in the refrigerator for as long as 2 weeks.

* See page 5.

United Arab Republic

To the foreigner, particularly one with a Western palate, there's a bit more to say about the archaeologic wonders of Egypt than about the food of the country. Basic patterns follow those of other Arabic countries, with a strong emphasis on lamb, mutton, yogurt and sweet fruits. Two interesting dishes are *Mlookhia,* a dish of chicken and greens, and *hareesie* (chicken with cracked wheat and spices). Breakfast is large, particularly in comparison to that of the U.A.R.'s neighbors in the same Mediterranean climate, and there's much nibbling between lunch and dinner on fruits, dates, figs and other little delicacies.

Mlookhia SERVES 6
210 calories per serving
(Chicken and Greens)

1 5-pound chicken, disjointed	2 teaspoons salt
1 onion	3 cloves garlic, minced
1 carrot	1 teaspoon ground coriander
2½ quarts water	2 tablespoons vegetable oil
2 pounds spinach, kale, or chard	

Put the chicken, onion, carrot and water in a saucepan. Cook over medium heat 2 hours, or until chicken is tender. Drain. Thoroughly wash, drain and dry the spinach or other greens. Chop coarsely. Pound salt, garlic and coriander to a smooth paste. Heat the oil in a saucepan and sauté the chicken and paste for 10 minutes. Add spinach and cook over medium heat 10 minutes. Taste for seasoning. Serve with cooked rice. The chicken broth may be strained and served separately.

NOTE: *Mlookhia* is the name of a popular Egyptian vegetable. The greens suggested are similar in flavor, though less bitter.

United Kingdom

For a civilized Western palate entering England for the first time it is important to remember not WHAT to eat but WHEN to eat. Their two best meals are breakfast and tea. Breakfast brings porridge, eggs, crunchy bacon or a kipper, toast and marmalade. For tea there's little sandwiches, crumpets, buns and scones. After that it's pretty much up to chance, for the other meals can be rough going, even following the roast beef and *Yorkshire pudding* route. England is a tea and beer drinking country, the beer most often served at room temperature in pubs which are sometimes quite historic and atmospheric.

Tea Cake SERVES 12 *100 calories per serving*

4 tablespoons butter or
margarine
½ cup low calorie granulated
sugar replacement*
2 egg yolks
2 tablespoons milk
2 teaspoons grated
orange rind

⅔ cup sifted cake flour
1 teaspoon baking powder
⅛ teaspoon salt
2 egg whites, stiffly beaten
2 tablespoons brown sugar
1 tablespoon cinnamon

Preheat oven to 375°. Lightly grease an 8-inch square pan.

Cream the butter; gradually add the sugar replacement, beating until light and fluffy. Add the egg yolks, milk and orange rind. Mix well. Sift the flour, baking powder and salt over the mixture, mixing until just blended. Fold in the beaten egg whites. Turn into the pan and sprinkle with the brown sugar and cinnamon mixed together.

Bake 20 minutes or until a cake tester comes out clean. Cool on a cake rack.

* See page 5.

Uruguay

A small republic with a hard currency from a big beef business is likely to have a lot of meat in the diet. It's true. Uruguayans, particularly the gauchos, consume a fantastic amount of beef. It's in all the usual recipes like *puchero* (mentioned under Argentina) and *pavesa* (rich beef broth), plus *asado con cuero* (beef barbecued in its own hide). In Montevideo fish specialties are popular, and *cazuela de pescado,* a baked fish in casserole, is quite delicious. Italian dishes are popular, both pastas and vegetables. Montevideo also sports a magnificent beach and many fine restaurants. *Maté,* a tea made from the leaves of the *Ilex paraguayensis,* is the national drink; however, as grapes grow well in Uruguay, they are being cultivated extensively and wine is becoming more and more popular.

Eggplant-Cheese Casserole   SERVES 6   *120 calories per serving*

1 large eggplant	½ teaspoon salt
boiling water	¼ teaspoon pepper
1 tablespoon olive oil	½ teaspoon minced garlic
½ cup dry bread crumbs	1 cup canned tomato sauce
3 tablespoons grated	3 thin slices mozzarella or
Parmesan cheese	white American cheese

Peel the eggplant and slice ¼-inch thick. Pour boiling water over the slices and let soak 5 minutes; drain and dry.

Heat the oil in a skillet; brown the eggplant slices on both sides.

Mix together the bread crumbs, cheese, salt, pepper and minced garlic. In a baking dish arrange layers of eggplant, bread-crumb mixture and the tomato sauce. Cover with the cheese.

Bake in a 325° oven 25 minutes.

Venezuela

Nature has been kind to Venezuela, endowing it with oil, a natural resource dear to modern man. Because of this wealth, much modernity can be found in cities like Caracas and Maracaibo, but the tropical interior remains largely untouched, with natives living and eating much the same way as they did centuries ago. Corn forms the basic diet in Venezuela and *mondongos* (soup-stews, similar to those of the Argentinian *puchero*) are great favorites. Unlike other South American countries, Venezuela makes breakfast a hearty meal; lunch and dinner are substantial too. Local cheeses are served plain or are used in desserts. Following the custom of their neighbors, dinner is served quite late, by our standards.

Chilled Cheese Cake   SERVES 10   *100 calories per serving*

2 teaspoons butter	½ cup low calorie granulated
¾ cup graham-cracker crumbs	sugar replacement*
3 cups cottage cheese	¼ teaspoon salt
2 tablespoons gelatin	1 tablespoon lemon juice
¾ cup water	1 teaspoon grated lemon rind
2 eggs, separated	1 teaspoon vanilla extract
¾ cup skim milk	½ cup nonfat dry milk

Rub the butter on the bottom and sides of an 8-inch spring-form pan. Press the cracker crumbs against it and chill while preparing the filling.

Force the cheese through a sieve. Soften the gelatin in ¼ cup water. Beat the egg yolks in the top of a double boiler. Add the milk, sugar replacement and salt. Place over hot water and cook, stirring constantly until thickened. Add the gelatin, lemon juice, rind and vanilla, continuing to cook, stirring until gelatin dissolves. Remove from the heat; cool 20 minutes, then stir in the cheese.

Beat the dry milk and remaining ½ cup water until the consistency of whipped cream. Beat the egg whites until stiff but not dry. Fold into the cheese mixture with the whipped milk. Turn into the spring-form pan. Chill until set—about 6 hours.

* See page 5.

Yugoslavia

Yugoslavia has many neighbors: Italy, Austria, Hungary, Romania, Bulgaria, Greece and Albania. Some of them have contributed to the Yugoslavian table, notably Romania, Bulgaria and Greece. A simple, hearty table it is. Yugoslavians are fond of onions, hot peppers, spicy pickles and other relishes with their lamb and mutton dishes. Other favorites are *cevapcici* (a beef-and-veal sausage) and *curka na pod varku* (turkey and sauerkraut) and Kebabs. After that, color Yugoslavian cuisine plum. Purple plum, that is. Plums, a favorite crop, are used in practically everything from preserves to soft drinks.

Yugoslavian Kebabs SERVES 6 *330 calories per serving*

1½ pounds lamb shoulder
 or leg
½ cup lemon juice
3 tablespoons grated onion
1 clove garlic, minced
2 teaspoons salt
¼ teaspoon diced ground
 red peppers
¼ teaspoon ground
 coriander
½ teaspoon turmeric
tomatoes
onions
green peppers
mushrooms
1 tablespoon olive oil

Trim the lamb of all fat; cut into 1-inch cubes. Mix together the lemon juice, onion, garlic, salt, red peppers, coriander and turmeric. Place the lamb in the mixture and let marinate for 2 hours, basting and turning the meat frequently.

Cut the tomatoes, onions and green peppers in pieces similar in size to the lamb. Thread the lamb and vegetables onto 6 individual skewers (no amount of vegetables is specified because the pieces of lamb will vary in number).

Place on an oiled broiling pan and broil in a hot broiler until browned on all sides. Turn the skewers frequently.

NOTE: The kebabs are delicious broiled over an open fire.

Calorie Chart

FOOD	SERVING	CALORIES

Breads

FOOD	SERVING	CALORIES
Bread crumbs	½ cup	165
Croutons	½" cubes	5
Melba toast	1 slice	20
Protein bread	¼" slice	30
Pumpernickel bread	½" slice	105
Raisin bread	½" slice	65
Rye bread	½" slice	55
Rye Krisp	1 piece	15
White bread	½" slice	65
Whole-wheat bread	½" slice	55

Dairy Products

FOOD	SERVING	CALORIES
American cheese	1 ounce	105
Bleu cheese	1 ounce	95
Brie cheese	1 ounce	100
Butter	1 tablespoon	100
Buttermilk, skim milk	1 cup	85
Camembert	1 ounce	85
Cheddar, processed	1 ounce	105
Cottage cheese	½ cup	105
Cream cheese	1 ounce	105
Cream, light	½ pint	490
Cream, heavy	½ pint	780
Edam cheese	1 ounce	120
Evaporated milk	1 tablespoon, unsweetened	25
Limburger	1 ounce	100
Milk, whole	1 cup	165
Milk, evaporated	1 cup	345
Milk, dried whole	1 tablespoon	39
Milk, dried skim	1 tablespoon	28
Parmesan cheese	1 ounce	110
Parmesan, grated	1 tablespoon	30
Pot cheese	1 tablespoon	30
Provolone cheese	1 ounce	105
Roquefort cheese	1 ounce	90
Sour cream	1 tablespoon	50
Swiss cheese	1 thin slice	100
Yogurt, skim milk	1 cup	115
Yogurt, whole milk	1 cup	180

Fish

Food	Serving	Calories
Bass	2″ x 2″ x 1″	100
Bluefish	2″ x 2″ x 1″	100
Butterfish	4 ounces	125
Brook trout, broiled	8 ounces	125
Cod	2″ x 2″ x 1″	90
Crab	4 ounces meat	100
Eel	4 ounces	125
Finnan Haddie	4 ounces	125
Flounder	2″ x 2″ x 1″	75
Haddock	2″ x 2″ x 1″	100
Halibut	2″ x 2″ x 1″	125
Herring, pickled	4 ounces	100
Herring, sour-cream	4 ounces	250
Lobster, 1 pound	4 ounces meat	100
Mackerel	2″ x 2″ x 2″	100
Salmon, broiled	3″ x 3″ x 1″	200
Salmon, smoked	4 ounces	325
Scallops	4 ounces	90
Shrimp	9 average	100
Sole, fillet of	4 ounces	90
Sturgeon, smoked	4 ounces	175
Swordfish	3″ x 3″ x ½″	225
Tuna, fresh	4 ounces	180
Whitefish	4 ounces	150

Fruits, Fresh

Food	Serving	Calories
Apples	1 medium	75
Apricots, fresh	1 medium	20
Apricots, dried	½ cup	200
Apricots, cooked	½ cup (with sugar)	240
Bananas	1 large	120
Blackberries, raw	1 cup	80
Blueberries, raw	1 cup	85
Cantaloupe	½, 5″ melon	40
Cherries, raw	1 cup unpitted	65
Coconut, fresh	1 cup shredded	350
Coconut, dried	4 ounce package	630
Fruit cocktail, fresh	½ cup	65
Grapefruit	½ medium, 4″	75
Honeydew melon	1 medium wedge	45
Lemon juice	1 tablespoon	4
Lemons	1 medium	20

Fruits, Fresh (Cont.)

Limes	1 medium	20
Nectarines	1 medium	40
Orange juice	1 cup	108
Oranges	1 medium	75
Peaches	1 medium	45
Pears	1 average	95
Pineapple, raw	1 slice, ½" thick	35
Plums	1 average	30
Pomegranate	1 average	75
Prunes	1 large	25
Raisins	1 cup	430
Raspberries, black	1 cup	100
Raspberries, red	1 cup	70
Strawberries	1 cup	55
Tangerines	1 medium	35
Watermelon	1 wedge, 4" x 8"	120

Meats and Poultry

Beef, boiled	4 ounces	200
Beef, ground	3 ounces	310
Beef, pot-roast	4 ounces	275
Beef, rib-roast	1 large slice	300
Beef, sirloin	3 ounces	260
Beef, stewing	average serving	325
Calf's liver	4 ounces	160
Chicken, broilers	½ average	330
Chicken, fried	4 ounces boneless	275
Chicken livers	4 ounces	150
Duck, roasted	4 ounces boneless	350
Lamb chop	4 ounces	350
Lamb, roast leg	3 ounces boneless	230
Lamb, shoulder	3 ounces boneless	290
Squab	1 average	275
Turkey	4 ounces	300
Veal cutlet, broiled	4 ounces boneless	210
Veal, shoulder	4 ounces	270

Vegetables

Asparagus	10 spears	25
Beans, green	1 cup	25
Beets	1 cup	70

Vegetables (Cont.)

Broccoli	1 cup	40
Brussels sprouts	1 cup	40
Cabbage, cooked	1 cup	40
Cabbage, raw	1 cup	25
Carrots	1 medium	20
Carrots, cooked	1 cup	45
Cauliflower	1 cup	30
Celery, cooked	1 cup	25
Celery, raw	1 large stalk	6
Chives	1 ounce	10
Cucumber	1 average	20
Endive	4 ounces	20
Garlic	1 clove	5
Lettuce	1 head	65
Mushrooms	1 cup	30
Olives, green	1	7
Olives, black	1	10
Onions, cooked	1 cup	80
Onions, green	10 large	100
Onions, raw	1 average	35
Parsley, chopped	1 tablespoon	1
Peas, cooked	1 cup	110
Peas, fresh	4 ounces in shell	115
Peppers	1 average	20
Pimientos	1 average	10
Potatoes	1 average	100
Radishes	10	25
Rice, boiled	1 cup	200
Rice, brown	½ cup raw	375
Rice, wild	½ cup raw	300
Scallions, young	6 small	25
Spinach, boiled	½ cup	50
Tomatoes	1 medium	25
Tomatoes, stewed	1 cup	50

Alcoholic Beverages

Beer	8 ounces	110
Bourbon whiskey	1 ounce	100
Brandy	1 ounce	80
Champagne, dry	4 ounces	110
Champagne, sweet	4 ounces	140
Cognac	1 ounce	80

Alcoholic Beverages (Cont.)

Gin	1½ ounces	125
Irish whiskey	1 ounce	100
Liqueurs	1 ounce	80
Manhattan	2½ ounces	250
Martini, dry	2½ ounces	180
Port wine	3½ ounces	100
Rum	1½ ounces	150
Rum and cola	tall glass	225
Rye whiskey	1 ounce	100
Scotch whiskey	1 ounce	100
Sherry, dry	3½ ounces	110
Sherry, sweet	3½ ounces	140
Vermouth, dry	1 ounce	40
Vermouth, sweet	1 ounce	60
Vodka	1½ ounces	125
Whiskey sour	3½ ounces	225
Wine, dry	3½ ounces	70
Wine, sweet	3½ ounces	125

Commercially Canned Foods (Average)

Vegetables

Asparagus	6 medium	20
Beans, baked	½ cup	140
Beans, green cut	½ cup	20
Beans, green lima	½ cup	75
Beets, cubed	½ cup	40
Carrots, cubed	½ cup	30
Mushrooms	½ cup	20
Peas, sweet	½ cup	60
Spinach	½ cup	20
Tomatoes	½ cup	25

Fish

Mackerel	½ cup	210
Salmon	½ cup	170
Sardines in oil	5 medium, drained	165
Sardines, tomato sauce	1½ large	225
Shrimp	10-12 medium	80
Tuna	½ cup, drained	255

Index